MASTERING YOUR MEAN GIRL

JEREMY P. TARCHER / PENGUIN
an imprint of Penguin Random House
New York

MASTERING YOUR

mean girl

The No-BS Guide to Silencing
Your Inner Critic and Becoming
Wildly Wealthy, Fabulously
Healthy, and Bursting with Love

MELISSA AMBROSINI

JEREMY P. TARCHER/PENGUIN
An imprint of Penguin Random House LLC
375 Hudson Street
New York, New York 10014

First published in Australia in 2016 by HarperCollins Publishers

First Tarcher/Penguin paperback edition published in 2016

Most Tarcher/Penguin books are available at special quantity discounts for bulk
purchase for sales promotions, premiums, fund-raising, and educational needs.
Special books or book excerpts also can be created to fit specific needs.
For details, write: SpecialMarkets@penguinrandomhouse.com.

ISBN 978-0-399-17671-5

Printed in the United States of America on recycled paper
7   9   10   8   6

Book design by Lauren Kolm

Some names and identifying characteristics have been changed to
protect the privacy of the individuals involved.

For my darling husband, Nick—you inspire me
every day to master my Mean Girl.

And for Leo, for reminding me daily to practice love.

I love you both immensely.

xx

contents

before we get started . . .

Hey, beautiful.

Thanks for picking up my book. I know you have a deep-down yearning for more—more happiness in your life, more health, more wealth, and more love. But there's one thing stopping you from living your wildest dreams and being the best version of yourself . . . your Mean Girl! Don't worry, I have one too.

How many times have you been in a roomful of people and felt paralyzed with worry, convinced that everyone else is judging you? How many times have you sabotaged yourself, just when you thought things were finally looking up? And how many times have you looked in the mirror and told yourself you were fat, stupid, ugly, unlovable, and worthless?

These moments are all examples of your Mean Girl at work.

You see, way too many beautiful, amazing women—just like you—

are living their lives paralyzed by fear. They're being held hostage by their inner critic, their Mean Girl, who rules their whole existence with an iron fist and an acid tongue. They end up crippled by comparison, stifled by self-criticism, and desperate to be loved.

I should know because my Mean Girl used to run my life.

It took me a long time to figure it out—via a pretty spectacular encounter with rock bottom—but here's what I now know to be true.

You don't need to be trapped by that fear-based Mean Girl voice inside your head—the one that constantly hisses that you're worthless and not good enough.

You don't need to live your life always worrying what other people think of you.

And you don't need to live your life constantly seeking permission, approval, and acceptance from others.

Deep down, I know you know this too. You're a smart and savvy woman with a yearning for something more; otherwise, you wouldn't have picked up this book. You know deep in your heart that there's a more inspiring, love-filled way to live. You know that it doesn't have to be the same old battle inside yourself, day in, day out.

I'm here to hold your hand, show you what's truly possible, and guide you back to your truth. There's no BS, no judgment, just plenty of real-life strategies and hard-won wisdom. It's all drawn from my own experiences, and it's all steeped in heartfelt love.

If you're ready to let go of the pain, sell your penthouse in Fear Town, and step into a new way of living, this book is for you.

This is not another "seven steps to enlightenment" book filled with self-help fluff and filler. It's not a glossy guide that simply rehashes the same old stuff you've read time and time again. And it's definitely not a quick-fix handbook that promises big results but leaves you feeling confused as to how to actually make it happen. This is a book filled with real wisdom that will get you real results. It's your no-BS road map to living your wildest dreams and becoming wildly wealthy, fabulously healthy, and bursting with love. If you take the information in the following pages and put it into practice every day, you'll be well on your way to mastering your Mean Girl and living your best life ever.

There are four things you need to know before we get started:

1. The principles in this book are how I actually live my life. I walk my talk: Every. Single. Day.
2. These ideas have been tried and tested, with profound results. Not only by me but also by the thousands of women I have worked with all over the world.
3. My mission is to support and inspire you, which is why I have created loads of complementary resources for you on my website **www.masteringyourmeangirl.com**. I encourage you to use them and I will indicate throughout the book where you can jump over to my site to get your goodies.
4. Most important of all, I am so excited to be sharing this knowledge and wisdom with you and helping you remember the truth of who you really are.

Learning how to master my Mean Girl quite literally changed my life. I know it will help you transform yours too.

Are you ready?

meet my mean girl—my story

"You can't write a book."

"Who do you think you are, Stephen King or something?"

"Don't you remember? Mrs. Bowman from year two called you stupid."

"Just spare yourself the pain and heartache—no one is going to read it, let alone buy it; no one cares what you have to say. It's going to be a flop."

"Stop now before you humiliate yourself."

Meet My Mean Girl

As I sat down to write this book—a blank white page staring me in the face—she reared her head with lightning speed, planting seeds of doubt and fear in my mind. In the past, it would have been enough to stop me in my tracks. To send me sprinting back quick smart to my comfort zone with a soothing chocolate bar and a glass of wine in hand. But because I now know the truth about her sneaky little games, I was able to take a different approach. Instead, I gently closed the door on her and returned to my truth—sharing the story that was sparking in my soul. This story.

I am not a guru, nor am I proclaiming to be enlightened. I'm just a regular woman who figured out how to master her Mean Girl and live the life of her dreams. There was no quick fix, no pill or magic potion, just pure determination and a yearning for something better, bigger, brighter.

It hasn't always been rainbows and butterflies, though. It took a pretty heavy wake-up call—where I hit rock bottom in spectacular fashion—for my life to change course. Mine is not your typical rags-to-riches story.

You see, life before I hit rock bottom was very different from now. I was a professional dancer at the Moulin Rouge in Paris and an actor, presenter, and occasional model. I worked on top-rated TV shows, performed on the world's biggest stages, and modeled for the best magazines. It might sound very exciting and "Hollywood," but it really wasn't. All that glitz and glamour is not what it's cracked up to be.

Let's Take It from the Top . . .

When I was three, my mother put me into dance classes. From the very beginning, I loved the freedom of jumping and swirling around with the music and expressing myself. As I got older, I started to get more serious about it. Pretty soon I was taking acting and singing classes as well, and by the grand old age of fifteen, I was working as a professional dancer and model while completing high school. I remember Mum picking me up from school and taking me straight to castings or to the studio. I would usually down a can of Coke, a packet of chips, and a chocolate bar to get me through the next four hours of dance classes, and I'd have to do my homework in the car or sitting in the studio waiting room until my next dance class started.

After high school I got accepted into university to study for a bachelor's degree in business. I had applied to appease my teachers and be like my peers, but I had never really been enthused about the thought of actually going through with it. So at age seventeen, with a strong desire to do things on my terms, I packed up and left home. I moved to a new city to follow my heart and study full-time at Brent Street, a professional development program in performing arts. I was so passionate about being on the stage; I just loved telling stories through movement and voice. I couldn't think of anything else I would rather do.

My parents were, and still are, incredibly supportive. They have always told me to follow my heart and do what feels right for me. They never interfered with what I was doing, even though their own work was miles away from performing. To this day I am extremely grateful for their continued love and support.

After I graduated from Brent Street, performing took me all over the world—to big cities such as Paris, London, and New York and all over Germany, Spain, New Zealand, and Australia. I became quite the jet-setter. I loved living out of a suitcase, being on a plane every few days, and the feeling of adventure and excitement that came with performing in a new place. But of course, it was only a matter of time before my Mean Girl got seriously involved.

When I lived in London I was attending up to seven castings and auditions per day and booking about 10 percent of them (pretty great stats, as any performer will tell you). Every time I walked out of a casting and didn't get the gig, I tried to take the sensible route and remind myself that there wasn't anything wrong with me—it's not you, they were just looking for a blonde, or someone who was taller or had blue eyes.

Nevertheless, it still hurt. In an industry where rejection is par for the course, you learn to develop a pretty thick skin. But even then, there's only so much you can take before it starts to eat away at you. After years of existing in this strange world of cattle calls and unexplained noes, I started to succumb more and more to the doubting thoughts inside me. I began to truly believe that I wasn't skinny enough, pretty enough, good enough, smart enough, whatever enough . . .

And you can probably guess what began to happen next.

Operation Self-Destruction

Throughout my career and life, I witnessed so many women look in the mirror and call themselves fat and ugly. Even the models and dancers who exemplified what movies, TV, and magazines told us real beauty was would still pinch the nonexistent "fat" on their thighs and screw up their faces in disgust. They would microscopically analyze every inch of their bodies and every pore on their faces while calling themselves the most awful names you can imagine. Thinking back, it breaks my heart, because if all these girls could see was imaginary flaws, how then could we expect anyone else to be happy in her own skin?

Being immersed in this environment planted a similar seed in my mind: Maybe I'm fat too. Maybe I'm not pretty enough either. Maybe I'm a worthless piece of crap as well.

From there, things escalated pretty quickly. I developed disordered eating habits, which I would battle for four years. I took up all sorts of unhealthy partying and binge drinking to distract myself from hunger and from the tumult growing inside me. I threw myself into work in an obsessive and destructive way. And I surrounded myself with relationships that weren't serving me—and I wasn't serving them either.

I also experienced my very first heartbreak. Up until then, I had always had nice boyfriends—very lovely, kind, and caring. This one, on the other hand, was . . . well . . . less than stellar. After a couple of years with him I found out he was cheating on me.

Being cheated on was awful, to say the least. I had never felt such heartache in all my life; the pain was excruciating. It felt like someone had ripped out my heart and fifty people were stomping on it while wearing six-inch stilettos. I was devastated, and I begged him to take me back—a telltale sign of the state of my self-esteem—but he didn't want me. (Who could blame him?) Within a week, I got scarily thin. I couldn't eat, sleep, or even work. All I did was lie in bed and cry. I couldn't stop thinking about it, about him. I sat in the suffering and hosted one giant pity party for myself. Nothing could lift my mood—my usual go-to fallbacks (chocolate and vino) were suddenly unappealing, and even a tempting night out on the town couldn't snap me out of it.

As well as nursing a broken heart, I also had to deal with the fact that my visa was about to expire, meaning I had to leave London (the place I had fallen deeply in love with) and move back home to Australia. My ex and I had planned to apply for a de facto visa together so I could stay in the country, and now that was out the window. I had to pack up my life, leave everything behind (my friends, my thriving career, the awesome pay), and head deep into the dark woods of the unknown. The Australian dance industry is pretty sleepy compared to the creative hotbeds of London and Paris, so I knew that moving home meant I'd be saying good-bye to that side of my career for good.

The gut-wrenching impact of all these factors left me reeling. I was so devastated and angry with myself for being hurt that I took what seemed to be the only sensible course of action in the circumstances: I closed off my heart. I completely shut down my emotional side so that I wouldn't get stung or blindsided like that ever again.

From then on, things got messy. I entered a series of toxic relationships because I didn't believe I was worthy of love. I had a heap of unhealthy friendships because I was scared to be alone. I exercised excessively because I wanted to fit in and be as skinny as the models in the magazines. I binged and purged and binged and purged, and then I did it again for good measure. I took drugs and drank alcohol to be "cool" and to be liked by my new "friends." And I accepted loads of lousy jobs that I hated just to make a buck and keep me afloat. I was one lost little kitten.

Everything I was doing in my life was coming from a space of scarcity, insecurity, and fear. I felt lost, completely disconnected from my truth, and I had no idea who the "real me" was anymore. The only thing I knew for sure was that the happy, free-spirited, bubbly girl I once had been was well and truly gone.

Hitting Rock Bottom—Hard

I spiraled into deep depression and started taking antidepressants. My body was sending me warning signs and screaming at me to *stop* and slow down, but I didn't listen. I suppressed my emotions with more drugs, alcohol, fast food, social media, gossip, toxic relationships, and TV. My body started shutting down. There was no more candle left to burn. The side effects from the medication were horrific, but—already unable to deal with day-to-day life—I simply ignored them. Instead, I suppressed the symptoms with more partying, dragged my unmotivated butt out of bed each morning, and kept pushing myself onward. The physical and emotional pain was debilitating, and there were days I wished I simply wouldn't wake up—they were the worst.

Of course, it was only a matter of time before my poor, exhausted body packed it in completely. Along with adrenal fatigue, thyroid problems, leaky gut, candida, high levels of mercury, serious hormonal imbalances, depression, an eating disorder, loads of vitamin and mineral deficiencies, adult acne and eczema all over my body, I suddenly developed a serious case of the cold sore virus (and I mean serious). I had cold sores all over my face, in my mouth, and down my throat—I couldn't eat, drink, talk, or even open my mouth, as the sores had made my lips stick together. As a friend was kind enough to point out, it looked like someone had taken a blowtorch to my face ... (Thanks!)

The cold sore virus landed me in the hospital in the end. I remember lying in the hospital bed with fluorescent lights buzzing overhead, thinking that this was it: my life was a mess, I felt like a mess, my health was a mess, and now I looked like a mess. Hi, Rock Bottom. Nice to meet you. My name's Melissa and my life officially sucks.

With hindsight I am grateful my wake-up call was this and not a more serious life-threatening illness, disaster, or the death of a loved one. And although this was by far the darkest point in *my* life, it was the turning point and wake-up call *I* needed to make some much-needed dramatic changes. And, no, you don't have to hit rock bottom (whatever that looks like for you) in order to turn your life around. You could have that internal moment on your yoga mat or driving in your car. It doesn't matter. All that matters is how you feel within yourself and how you take action every day to live a happier and healthier life.

Looking back, it was such a pivotal moment, because the one thing that I needed in order to work was my body, and all of a sudden that was no longer functioning. I was learning the hard way: without your health, you have nothing.

At first it felt like a cruel joke. But looking back, I know it was the Universe trying to get through to me: you aren't living your truth, sweetheart, and you aren't paying attention to all the signs to stop and listen—so I'm going to have to *make* you stop. Ah, the Universe works in such crafty ways!

Finally I got the lesson, and I heard the calling for something deeper within my core. With every fiber of my being I knew that the career path I was following—and the lifestyle that went with it—wasn't right for me. I knew the people I was surrounded by weren't serving me, and I knew the food I was (and wasn't) eating wasn't of the highest vibration. Of course, that still didn't mean that things changed straightaway. My Mean Girl wasn't going to let me off the hook and leave my career without a fight, and I still had a whole heap of learning to do. But the seeds of change had definitely been planted.

The first book I picked up in the hospital was Louise Hay's classic *You Can Heal Your Life*. That was when things began to click. It was like all the messed-up puzzle pieces inside my head started to slide into place and all my health problems suddenly made sense. From then on I became obsessed with the personal-development world, metaphysics, holistic health, and learning about how to understand and be my unique self—something that was so foreign to me. I read every book I could get my hands on, immersing myself in the wisdom of great teachers like Eckhart Tolle, Deepak Chopra, Louise Hay, the Dalai Lama, and Marianne Williamson.

I realized a few potent truths while lying in that hospital bed with no distractions . . .

- I realized I was the reason I was lying there.
- I realized I had no idea how to look after myself or what the heck this self-love business was that Louise Hay was talking about.
- I realized I had to take responsibility for my own health and happiness and that the decision to live my best life lay with me.

I realized I had to stop looking outside myself to find happiness and start connecting with my inner self— my truth, my spirit, my soul essence.

Since then I have been on a rewarding inward journey back to my truth, which is love. After years of learning, reading, studying, experimenting, falling over, getting back up, and trying again, I can now confidently say that I have mastered my Mean Girl. I have overcome the negative patterns that were keeping me so sick, stuck, and unhappy. Instead, I have carved out a heart-centered life that is authentic to me, that lights me up from deep within, and that fills my chest with heart-thumping joy.

My journey is far from over, though—I choose to keep learning, growing, and evolving every day. I choose to keep mastering my Mean Girl every second. And I continue to choose love over fear in every moment and to remind myself that we only have this one precious life—so let's make the most of it!

But even though I'm still evolving (and am definitely not "perfect"), life these days is very different. Like, beyond-my-wildest-dreams different.

Every morning I pinch myself while jotting down the things I am grateful for: I am married to my soul mate, Nick; I have the most divine stepson imaginable, Leo; I have a thriving career and business that fulfills me and is helping women live their best life; I am surrounded by relationships that inspire the heck out of me; my heart is full to the brim with love; and I am the strongest and healthiest I have ever been in my life. It's safe to say I am wildly wealthy, fabulously healthy, and bursting with love. Now I want to show you how you can master your inner Mean Girl and experience a love-filled life too. Because I am a regular girl, just like you. I am no more "special" than you. I've just had the courage to choose differently. And you can too! Yes, I have had privileges such as being born in Australia to a middle-class family. I have supportive parents and four working limbs. I understand there are obstacles that can get in your way—however, the biggest obstacle is your Mean Girl.

Although I've studied many different philosophies and schools of thought, I'm definitely not here to preach. This is not about imparting harsh guidelines or telling you what you should and shouldn't do. And it's definitely not a "my way or the highway" book of rules and regulations.

I'm here to be your bestie, hold your hand, and share my journey and what I have learned along the way with you. Everything within these pages you already know at a deep-down level, but along your odyssey through life someone told you you weren't smart enough, or you had your heart broken, or you were bullied, hurt, laughed at, or told to stop or that you were stupid, which all resulted in you closing off a little bit of that beautiful heart of yours. But it's now time to open it back up! I simply want to inspire you to remember the truth of who you really are, to master your inner Mean Girl, and to live your dream life.

Because, darling, when you do, everything changes. And life—to be frank—starts to freaking rock.

Are you ready, gorgeous?

Let's do this.

PART ONE

Make Love Your Internal GPS

ONE

choose love over fear

I believe that every single event in life happens
in an opportunity to choose love over fear.

OPRAH WINFREY

What Is Your Mean Girl?

Your Mean Girl = your ego.

To put it simply, your Mean Girl is that voice inside your head
that is constantly feeding your negative chatter. She lives in a per-
petual state of fear and is always telling you you're not good enough,
smart enough, pretty enough, wealthy enough, wise enough, brave
enough, or successful enough. (Hot tip: don't listen to her!)

Some teachers call this voice the ego, the inner critic, the voice,
but I prefer to call it your "Mean Girl" (or "Mean Boy" for the fellas).
Because all of us can relate to the harsh, judgmental voice of the bul-
lies who sat behind us in high school and the painful sting of their
words. Using this metaphor also gives us a rude wake-up call: we
realize we have our very own self-created bully living inside our
heads every minute of the day. Regardless of what language you

use to describe it, your Mean Girl/ego is not your true self. She's all about judgment, labels, comparison, roles, masks, expectations, fear, and fitting into a neat little box . . . none of which is the truth of who you really are.

There are no exceptions when it comes to the Mean Girl—we've all got this nasty little voice in our heads. Even self-help gurus, Zen masters, and the Dalai Lama have an inner critic planting seeds of doubt. The only difference between the Dalai Lama and your average person on the street is that he's learned how to master his Mean Boy—his ego is on mute. It's there, but he gives it absolutely no power and no airtime.

The good news is that all of *us* can learn how to master our inner fear-based voice too. Yep, that includes you. I'm the definitive proof it can be done—if I can do it, then so can you. Until I figured out how to master her, my Mean Girl was on max volume with a very heavy bass. She ran the show, called the shots, and basically ruled the roost. But guess what? . . . I let her. Why? Because I didn't know there was any other way to live. I had not yet rediscovered the truth that would change everything for me: *that love is my—and all of our— natural state of being.*

Yep, *love.*

Sounds a little woo-woo, huh? It's the truth, though. You see, we are born into this world as whole, beautiful, overflowing-with-love tiny beings. As gorgeous little bubbas, all we know is presence— we're not distracted by thoughts of what's going to come next, we're not worried about the past, and we're definitely not stressing about what other people think of us. We have no reference to the past or future, only the present moment. All we know is that when we're hungry, we cry. When we're tired, we sleep (or scream). And when we're happy, we smile our big, gummy grins.

In that perfect present state, we are the embodiment of love. Usually there's someone there who will hug us, comfort us, and feed us when we're hungry. We don't have to do anything to earn that love: just by our mere state of being and existing, that love is ours. Love is all we know.

Then along our journey through life, we get conditioned to think otherwise. By age three, we've already been told the word "no" thousands of times. At eight, someone calls you stupid and it sinks into your psyche. At thirteen, the school bully throws her lunch at you and calls you fat, which you then believe to be true. At fifteen, your parents get divorced and you blame yourself. At eighteen, you have your first heartbreak, which makes you think you're undesirable. At twenty-two, you get fired from your job and start believing you're now unemployable and stupid. At twenty-five, you travel overseas and accumulate ten thousand dollars' worth of debt, which you then let hang over you and dictate your every move.

It's enough to convince even the strongest people that they're worthless and unlovable. In fact, that's exactly what happens to almost all of us, even if our journeys are really different from the one I just described. But the truth is, although these things that happen along our journey might influence and shape us—not to mention hurt us—they don't actually define us. They are just stories from the past we keep telling ourselves.

Soul Share

Soul Shares are little whispers of love to nudge you back onto your path. They'll be popping up throughout this book and are designed to be short, sweet, and very potent. I encourage you to really embrace their wisdom by writing them down on Post-it Notes, sharing them on social media, sticking them on your vision board, writing them in lipstick on your bathroom mirror, setting them as reminders in your phone, or tattooing them on your forehead . . . just kidding about that last one. But seriously, use them as constant reminders to guide you back to your truth. Their simple, intuitive wisdom is profoundly powerful.

There is also a collection of beautifully designed Soul Share graphics available on my website for free, ready for you to download, print, pin, share, and inspire. Head over to www.masteringyour meangirl.com to get yours.

And now, for our first Soul Share . . .

Let me drop a truth-bomb on you:

> ### Soul Share
>
> You are not your circumstances,
> your experiences, or your past.

Although you may feel like they make up who you are, you're actually so much bigger than that. You are nothing short of a pure miracle and the embodiment of love. This is your truth! This is the nature of who you really are. Not the life experiences that have beaten you down. Not the crowning achievements that have boosted you up. And not the limiting, fear-based chatter that runs through your mind on a daily basis.

You are the embodiment of love and you simply being here is a miracle.

Your life experiences, however, serve an important role in your evolution. They're an opportunity for growth and a chance to return back to love—your natural state. But that's all. Don't use your life experiences as a way to define yourself. And *don't* let them become ammunition for your Mean Girl.

I could have easily let the fact that I had my heart broken dictate my future relationships—and indeed I did for many years, repeating old patterns and stinky habits. But then I realized I no longer needed that old chapter to be part of my current reality, so I let it go. I decided not to let those past experiences continue shaping and affecting my future.

Inspo-action

Because information is useless without inspired action, you will see loads of inspo-actions throughout this book to help you really implement your learnings.

Take a moment now and write down a few experiences

or stories you are holding on to that are no longer serving you. Maybe it's the fact that your parents got divorced when you were five or that you got sick or fired or you flunked out of university. Whatever comes up for you, write it down in detail.

_____

_____

_____

_____

_____

Now comes the powerful part: put a line through each experience. If you wrote it out on a piece of paper, you can rip it up and stick it in the trash. (And if you're a fan of ritual, you could even burn your piece of paper—somewhere safe, of course!) Now that you are aware of the old stories you have continued to tell yourself, I invite you to let go of them and catch yourself next time you automatically go to bring them up.

Awareness is key when it comes to reprogramming your thought patterns and mastering your Mean Girl. It takes time and commitment to cement the change, but you can do it! All it needs is a willingness to be your highest self and to choose love. So next time you go to press play on an old story, stop! Take a breath, let it go, and choose to come back to the present moment instead. And remember, once you are aware of something, you can't unknow it—the seeds of change have already been planted and you'll get there in the end.

"Ego" Is Not a Dirty Word

There are many spiritual texts, teachers, and gurus who talk about smashing your Mean Girl/ego, but I believe when she comes knocking to plant fear in your mind you have to accept that she is part of you and become besties with her. Now, becoming besties doesn't mean you invite her in for a cuppa and she ends up sleeping over and wearing your clothes for the next three months. Oh no! Your Mean Girl is part of you, embedded so deeply that many people aren't even aware of her wily ways and shifty presence. Awareness is the key to mastering your Mean Girl, because once you know what you know, you can't unknow it. So rather than fighting her, slamming the door in her face, and resisting her every step of the way, it's more constructive to use her as a guide back to your truth . . . love! It's the difference between getting angry and confrontational when she comes knocking, and gently closing the door on her and using her as a trigger to choose love instead. There's a big difference.

As you will discover later in this book, it's this simple decision to choose love over fear on a moment-to-moment basis that becomes the framework for your internal GPS system. Make no mistake: this one simple shift in how you operate will absolutely change your life forever.

Love versus Fear

In every moment you have one of two choices: you can choose either love or fear—your truth or your Mean Girl. This simple choice underpins every decision you make throughout the day, from what you choose to put in your mouth, to how you respond to the person who cuts you off at a traffic light. From how you move your body, to the people you surround yourself with. From what you do with your time, to how you treat yourself. It all comes down to choice . . . your choice.

One of my favorite personal development texts, *A Return to Love* by Marianne Williamson, says a miracle is a shift in perception from fear to love. My mission is to help you live a miraculous life far greater than your wildest dreams, but in order for me to help you do that you will need to choose love over fear in every moment.

Of course, sometimes we don't even realize we're making a choice, but we are all the time. Before my giant wake-up call, I was making some pretty lousy choices about how I lived my life without even being aware of them. I was choosing to suffer, to live in a constant state of fear, and I gave all my power away to other people. I thought the world was against me, and, as a result, every decision and action reflected that belief.

- I took jobs I hated and held on with a tight grip to every dollar I had out of fear of not having enough money.
- I flogged my body at the gym out of fear of getting fat, and I ate (or didn't eat) out of hatred for what I looked like in the mirror.
- I surrounded myself with unhealthy "friends" and put up with a series of unhealthy relationships out of fear of being rejected.
- I "people pleased" because I was scared of disappointing others.

≈ I partied and trashed my body on the weekends to numb the deep loneliness I felt within.

≈ Basically, I believed that the world was a dark, dangerous place and I barely deserved to be in it.

If these sorts of thinking patterns sound painfully familiar to you, don't worry. You're not alone. It doesn't mean you're weird or that you've got faulty programming or that you missed out on a key piece of the life puzzle. The thing is, we're never taught how to think with anything but a fear-based mentality. At school we're never shown how to master our mind and make peace with our Mean Girl. Our parents weren't taught it, nor were our grandparents, nor the leaders and trailblazers we admire. In fact, fear-based thinking has become hardwired into the operating system of modern society. But what if we could turn it all around? Imagine a class at school on self-love, meditation, nourishing your body, caring for the planet, conscious movement, mindful eating, creative expression, earthing, entrepreneurship, compassion, grounding, authenticity, respecting Mother Nature, and practicing gratitude. How amazing would that be? Sign me up, baby!

There is an epidemic of fear: it's the state in which we all live. But you'll soon see that turning your back on the old paradigm and choosing love instead of fear is not only possible, it's essential and super easy.

Better yet, once you master the art of choosing love over fear, it will place your dream life at your fingertips.

Inspo-action

It's time to get super honest with yourself. What are you currently doing in your life out of love?

_____

_____

_____

_____

_____

What are you doing out of fear?

_____

_____

_____

_____

Now that you are aware of what you are doing out of love and what you are doing out of fear, I invite you to catch yourself next time you go to do something out of fear and switch it over to love instead. This will take practice (like anything worth working for), but keep at it.

The Road Back from Rock Bottom

We accept the love we think we deserve.

STEPHEN CHBOSKY, *The Perks of Being a Wallflower*

I believe everything we are dealt in life is an opportunity for growth. Even the deep, dark, painful stuff. There are lessons, messages, and nuggets of wisdom in every experience. Our job is to open our awareness, find the nugget, and embrace the learning. Because if we don't, the same lesson will come back around again in two weeks, two years—maybe even two decades—until we manage to get the message.

Making the mental shift to see the opportunity for growth in the tough stuff is hard. It means you have to start taking responsibility, and most people hate thinking that they're responsible for the crappy things in their life. We're happy to lap up the praise when we kick goals, but when things fall to pieces we are quick to point the finger and blame others. Taking self responsibility isn't easy and it means you have to start taking action and owning how you show up in the world. Not to mention stop pointing the finger and blaming everyone else . . . Scary stuff, I know. But remember that old saying—every time you point the finger at someone else, there are three fingers pointing right back at you. It may be trite, but it's true.

When I realized I had to start taking responsibility for my own happiness and could no longer blame other people—like my parents, my ex-boyfriend, or Mrs. Bowman—for the way my life had turned out, it was an incredibly tough pill to swallow. I didn't want to accept it. In fact, without my spectacular crash-and-burn, I don't know if I would have accepted it at all. In all likelihood, I'd still be battling along—treating my body like crap, struggling to be an actor even though I didn't love it anymore, and dating men who treated me like a doormat. I'd take rock bottom over a lifetime of that any day.

I have to be honest with you, though: after I landed my butt in the hospital I didn't get the hint straightaway. I still chose fear instead of love many times and continued to struggle with the consequences.

After my face healed from all the cold sores, eczema, and acne and I got my strength back, I jumped straight back into acting. Why? Because it was "safe." It was what I knew. It was my comfort zone. But I soon realized there was no true comfort in that zone, only discomfort, uneasiness, and a whole lot of fear. As always, the Universe was three steps ahead of me. Every time I got a job—whether it was the day before the shoot, during the shoot, or just after they called "cut"—I would end up with a faceful of cold sores, my immune system down, collapsed in the emergency department or doctor's office and loaded up on drugs for weeks.

Notable examples of this "fun" cycle happened after I landed small roles on two major TV shows, *Home and Away* and *Packed to the Rafters*. My Mean Girl was so excited to get the gigs, but when I finally made it onto the set I felt empty. I was still so confused by my feelings—getting on Australia's most popular TV shows was meant to be "it," the pinnacle of my career—but I felt utterly drab and lifeless. My passion for acting was no longer there, and I hadn't yet realized that I was just doing it because it was safe and what I was used to. I'd been performing since I was three years old—there wasn't anything else I could do, right? I finished the gigs feeling flat, unfulfilled, and deflated. Like clockwork, I broke out in my usual bumps, blemishes, cold sores, and pustules; my immune system shut down; and I went back on the antidepressants, steroids, antibiotics, antivirals, and anything else the doctors threw at me (which only made me feel worse).

So do you think I had learned my lesson yet? Not quite.

My face healed and I went at it again. I landed another huge gig as the face of a big campaign. For this job they flew me to New Zealand to film the promotion. I had to look elegant while bungee jumping (my first time!) and deliver my lines in a bikini in the middle of the chilly New Zealand winter. As you can imagine, as soon as they said "cut," my body knew it could finally let go. I got on the plane sick, with a face full of cold sores, and spent the next three weeks in bed dosed to the max.

Finally, finally, lying in bed, I vowed to let go of this life that was hurting me so much. With hindsight, I can clearly see that acting wasn't my truth. It always felt hard, as if I was trying to fit a square peg in a round hole.

But it's no easy feat to let go of a dream (and identity) you've held for most of your life. I had built my self-worth around what I did for a living. I had let it define me, so when I finally cut the cord and closed the door, I entered a full-blown identity crisis. If I wasn't an actor, dancer, and model, who the hell was I? It wasn't until much later that I realized my work does *not* define me. Yes, it may be something I love and a beautiful form of self-expression, but it is not who I am. I am love.

At the time of my identity crisis, I was living at my friend's flat, sleeping on a fold-out single bed in her lounge room (for free— bless her!). I was strapped for cash and had no idea what I was going to do with myself or my life. All I knew was that the life I was living was not serving me. But what to do instead?

I remember calling one of my lifelong besties, Cassie, who gave me some much-needed tough love: "Get up, get out of bed, and sort your life out."

I began getting help and doing some soul searching to figure out what I was passionate about. I was so disconnected from myself that I didn't know the answer to that simple question straight off the bat. The thing that kept popping up in my mind was helping women with their health and their lives. With all the crapola my body was going through, I had become absolutely fascinated with the idea of turning to Mama Nature to help it heal. I realized that your emotions and what you eat are deeply interconnected, and I wanted to help others become happy and healthy. It was the topic that I most often found myself Googling and buying books about—it seemed as good a place as any to start a new career.

When I was in the hospital I reached out to the late Jess Ainscough, a.k.a. The Wellness Warrior, who quickly became a soul sister. I was so inspired by her and the fact that she embraced both natural and conventional medicine to support her on her cancer journey. The way Mother Nature had supported her inspired me to get off my medications and sort my health and life out. She also inspired me to study holistic nutrition at the Institute for Integrative Nutrition. The course intrigued me and it seemed like an excellent stepping-stone to get me back on my feet. It was unlike anything I'd ever studied before and I couldn't afford the tuition, but my mind was made up.

With absolutely no idea what I was going to do with the certification, how I was going to make a living at the end of it, or how I was even going to get clients, I simply decided to follow my heart.

That moment was the first time I chose love over fear despite my circumstances.

What Is Love?

Masters are those who have chosen only love. In every instance.
In every moment. In every circumstance.

NEALE DONALD WALSCH, *Conversations with God*

Fast-forward a few years. In February 2015, I found myself sitting at Jess's house on the phone to her local florist ordering flowers for her funeral. This wasn't the plan, God damn it! I was meant to be sitting next to her ordering flowers for her wedding in a few months' time. But the Universe had a different plan for this angel. And although there was pain (and still is, for that matter), I am so truly grateful for the time we got to share and I feel okay now knowing she is dancing in the clouds.

Losing my best friend at twenty-eight years old allowed me to experience feelings I never knew were humanly possible. I was cracked wide open and had my heart ripped out of my chest, shattered into a million pieces, and then put back in. It tested me and pushed me to really step up and practice everything I teach. I allowed myself to grieve fully and completely, and with the support of my darling husband—who would hold me for hours as I wept my heart out—I was able to express myself truthfully in every moment.

Throughout that experience, I observed the waves of different emotions washing over me, knowing that I was not that emotion. I allowed my body to fully feel everything that needed to be felt. It was challenging and stretched me to my limits, but it made me a better, more resilient person. Exactly what Jess would have wanted.

You see, Jess was and still is one of my biggest teachers. She taught me so many things—how to follow my dreams, how to tread more lightly with myself (and the planet), how to live a life of passion and purpose, and even how to do a coffee enema (!). Now, every day, she reminds me on an even deeper level that *I am love*, that love is all around me, that my truth is love, and that you can close your eyes and in an instant return back to love. It truly is the greatest gift.

The power lies in its ability to spring us back to our truth—love. Love is our natural state, our birthright, and when we learn to live in alignment with it, life starts to flow a lot more effortlessly. In fact, when you choose love you'll find you're living a life greater than your wildest dreams.

However, if you've been operating with a fear-based mentality for a long time, it can be tricky to know what living from a place of love actually feels and looks like. We can start to think that if we don't have the Hollywood version of love—complete with red roses and Prince Charming coming to rescue us—then we don't have love ... But that couldn't be further from the truth.

You know those times when you are "in flow," as Mihaly Csikszentmihalyi calls it—there isn't a thought in your mind; time flies by in a split second; your whole self is completely engaged in the moment; you feel deeply connected, whether to others, yourself, nature, or the Universe at large; opportunities present themselves effortlessly; and serendipity becomes the norm? That's what it can be like when you choose love over fear.

And what about that feeling of deep peace that fills your whole body—perhaps when you're with people you care about, or when you're blissed out on your yoga mat in savasana or you're deep in a juicy meditation or you're wrapped in the arms of your honey? Yep, that's flow too.

As you can see, love is so much more than just the romantic choccies-and-flowers type of business you see in the movies. It's way more all encompassing and universal than that. If you're still having trouble distinguishing what love is and feels like, it can actually be easier to identify the times when you're *not* living from a space of love. Basically, anytime that you're stressed over the past, you're worrying about the future, or you feel anxious, angry, indecisive, or not present, it can mean you're spending too much time hanging out in Fear Town and sipping cocktails with your Mean Girl and are not in the here and now. And don't get me wrong: feeling those feelings is going to happen (on a daily basis, I might add) and in some cases is totally warranted. However, it's how you deal with them and how quickly you return to love that matters most.

The brilliant thing is that once you're aware of the difference, it's a simple choice to shift your internal GPS and return back to love.

Your Internal GPS

A GPS is a navigation system that guides you to exactly where you want to go. Whether you've been somewhere before or are going there for the first time, you simply plug in the little device and *bam*— you end up at your destination.

But what's an internal GPS?

This is the navigation system inside you that leads you to where you want to be. Like a compass that always points due north or the evening star that never fails to guide you home.

When you set up your internal GPS in a way that serves you, it'll always lead you home to your truth—yep, you guessed it, love. However, when you bombard the system with too much interference (read: fear-based Mean Girl chatter), it becomes much harder to tune in to the innate wisdom of your GPS and you're likely to be sent astray.

If you want to shift your state to one of love and really hardwire your GPS system to guide you toward that truth, there's one simple question you need to go back to. You guessed it . . .

What would love do right now?

This question will guide you back to your truth, back to your natural state, back to your essence. Every. Single. Time.

If you're serious about living from love, this isn't a question you can ask just once or twice and you're done with it; it's an ongoing process. A continual recalibration and realignment to ensure that your inner compass is always angled at true north. And it can be applied to every situation and conundrum you can think of, from the spiritual to the mundane to the crazily chaotic.

Case in point? My wedding. Let's face it: weddings usually bring out the crazy in people. In fact, no one blinks an eye when the doting wife-to-be turns into a raving Bridezilla—definitely not the most loving way to head into matrimony. But for my own big day, I was determined to plan and carry out the entire event with nothing but love in my heart and ease and grace as my intention.

As I was organizing the wedding, I had loads of people giving me their opinions on how they thought my big day should be. For Old Melissa, this might have ruffled her feathers and sparked her ego—*This is my day. Don't tell me what to do!* But Post-Rock-Bottom Melissa was able to simply check in with her internal GPS and ask herself what the wedding was actually about for her. The answers came flooding in, thick and fast. This wedding is about celebrating my darling and me finding each other again in this lifetime. It's about celebrating our love. It's about uniting as one. It's about sharing our love. Most important of all, it's about the two of us and the love we have for each other.

So every time someone told me that I simply had to invite so-and-so, or that I simply must have *x*, *y*, and *z*, I was able to turn to my inner compass instead. Rather than chucking a tantrum and throwing my toys out of the pram, I asked myself: how would love respond? For me, the answer was clear. Love would open its heart and respond to every well-intentioned piece of advice with this: "Thank you so much for your great suggestion; I have taken it on board and appreciate your input."

In that moment, I put out the fire with love. A different answer could have sent things up in flames. My adviser and I could have not spoken for months or even years. It could have been disastrous. But instead, any tension was dissolved and the input was received with the utmost love. Because I spoke from my heart I reached the other person's heart, but if I had spoken from my head, I would have gotten an egoistic response back.

You see, as with almost everything in life, *it's not about being right or wrong—it's about who showed up with love. In any moment, in any situation, you can dissolve any conflict with love.*

One of my clients, Tracy, came to me at the point of wanting to divorce her husband. After teasing out the details, it seemed to all boil down to her not feeling heard by him. I advised her to sit down with him, open her heart, and share how she was truly feeling. She thought he would get angry, but because she spoke from a place of love, it was received with love. He said he'd had no idea she was feeling that way and committed to showing up more and really making an extra effort. It could have been an inflammatory conversation, but because Tracy had come from a place of love within herself first (before she went to her husband), they managed to have a true heart-to-heart exchange, and that one conversation saved their marriage. They are still together, happier than ever, and practice speaking and communicating from a place of love, every single day.

(I've changed most of the names and identifying features of people—like Tracy—mentioned in this book—to protect their privacy.)

The same applies when you're with your kiddies. Whenever I chat with Leo—my gorgeous stepson—about the importance of eating his greens and cleaning up after himself, if I do it from a place of love, it is usually received with love and acted on almost immediately. The times when I am angry and not acting as my highest self, we both get riled up and walk away feeling unheard and unhappy.

Love over Fear Exercise

Can you think of a time recently when you have approached a conversation with someone you care about out of fear, when you could have turned it around and acted out of love instead? Write down your experience, in particular noting how you felt before, during, and after the exchange.

_____

_____

_____

_____

_____

Next time something comes up that would usually trigger a fear-based reaction from you, I invite you to gently return back to your heart and choose love instead. This simple yet powerful action will dramatically change your relationships and can affect the course of your entire life.

Love Trumps Fear Every Time

Picture this: You're in a concrete jail cell. There are no windows or doors, just four concrete walls around you, a ceiling above, and a floor under your feet. It's pitch-black and you can't see a thing. Now you light a match. With that one small strike, you illuminate the entire room and you can now see the tiny hole, just big enough for you to crawl out. There is so much darkness, yet there's no doubt that the radiant ball of light in your hands is stronger than the shadows, no matter how small the match is.

Light is love. Dark is fear.

Don't ever forget that your light is more powerful than your darkness. Although at times it may not feel like the case, remember this jail cell analogy and remind yourself that all you need is to connect with that light within you to find your way out.

When you go through difficult times in your life, it's easy to believe that the light inside you has been snuffed out. We've all gone through periods of intense fear—maybe you've been hurt, someone you deeply love has died, you found out you have a serious illness, or you've lost the very roof over your head. But don't let your darkness stop you from shining your light. It can absolutely be dispersed by love, if you let it.

Let it be said, though, this isn't about glossing over what has happened to you. You need to fully and completely feel the pain, anger, frustration, and sadness—and I am going to teach you exactly how to do that later—but you do *not* need to let it ruin or dictate your life. Feeling the emotions bubbling inside you is an important part of your healing process and not one to be skipped over. Embrace it and ride the wave.

For me, Jess's passing was one of the hardest things I have ever experienced. There were moments when I questioned everything about my existence and wondered what the hell the point of life was. But although the pain was immense, I knew it was all part of the process. I knew that "this too shall pass."

No matter how utterly sad I felt or how much my heart hurt, I was also keenly aware of something else too: a rainbow is made up of all different colors. For a rainbow to be a rainbow, all the colors need to be there; you can't skip over certain colors or leave one out altogether. As I witnessed the entire spectrum of emotions wash over me, again and again (sometimes seemingly all at once), I tried to visualize them as the bands of a rainbow. I knew they all had to be there, and I tried not to judge them or get stuck in them.

I know that I could have easily let all that darkness swallow me whole. I truly believe that my commitment to letting myself feel what was necessary without trying to fight it or block it was what kept my grief at the "healthy" end of the spectrum and allowed me to keep journeying through the heartbreak till I wound up back at a place of love and gratitude.

The most powerful thing you can do, then, in any situation, even at your lowest depths and the darkest moments when you're consumed by fear, is to recommit to the spark of love inside you. It's always there, it's always burning, and it will always guide you back to your truth.

Inspo-action

Where in your life are you choosing fear instead of love? Be honest with yourself and take the following quiz to help you identify any areas in your life that might need an injection of TLC.

In each row, circle the option that is most relevant for you, then tally up how many results you get in each column.

love vs. fear

I exercise because I love the way it makes me feel.	I exercise because I hate the size of my bum and thighs and because I'm desperate to fit into my jeans again.

I eat because I honor my temple and want to give it the best-quality nourishment I can.	I limit and restrict what I eat out of fear of getting fat.
The people who surround me are loving, supportive, and aligned with my beliefs.	I am holding on to toxic relationships because I am scared I will have no friends.
I am with my partner because I simply love to be with this person.	I am with my partner because it's convenient for now and I don't want to be alone.
I do work that I find love and joy in.	I go to an uninspiring job that I don't enjoy or like.
I see money as energy and don't let it control my life.	I am in debt and can never get on top of my finances.
I regularly take time for myself to sit in stillness, turn inward, and reflect.	I don't have the time and I can't bear the thought of stopping and sitting with myself and my feelings.
I believe we are here to be our unique selves and to be of service to others.	I am not contributing in any way to the world.

I turn to Mother Nature to help support and nourish my body.	I take the quick option when I am unwell—a pill or potion that I might not need, but will instantly make me feel better.
I don't pollute my body because I love my beautiful temple too much.	I take drugs and drink alcohol regularly, even though I know deep down it's not my truth.

___out of 10   ___out of 10

How did you score?

You are looking to achieve the highest score possible in the Love column, and as low as possible in the Fear column. Check back in regularly by redoing this quick quiz to see how you are progressing.

Now that you are aware of which areas in your life you are living out of fear, ask yourself how you can reframe the items in the Fear column so they're rooted in love. What is the truth behind each fear? Are there any fears you can release right now?

If there are a few things in your Fear column, don't worry. I know it can seem overwhelming, but just start with one area first. For example, just start by choosing to eat out of love. Try that for two weeks and see how you feel. After that you can move on to the next area. Again check in with yourself after the two weeks, see how you feel, then try something else.

The great thing is that when you start making changes in one area of your life, a ripple effect occurs. So often with my clients, I would see them try really hard in one area, only to all of a sudden start experiencing shifts in other areas as well—almost effortlessly.

For example, one beautiful client, Sam, decided she wanted to start by focusing on moving her body out of love first. After a few weeks, she realized she was more inclined to reach for healthier food options, she was more excited about going to yoga on Saturday morning than Friday night drinks, her Mean Girl wasn't as loud as usual, and she was gravitating to more inspiring people at work. It's pretty cool what can start to unfold when you choose love!

If taking it one area at a time isn't your style, you can choose to go cold turkey like my client Kate. When we started working together she decided she wanted to completely ditch the fear-based living and switch her internal GPS system over to love all at once. As she's a very "all or nothing" type of person, this route suited her completely, but the choice is totally up to you. See what feels right in your heart and do that.

Use this as your guide, and whenever your Mean Girl nudges you to choose fear, simply remind her you are going to choose love instead.

Choosing Love over Fear Recap

- Every decision comes down to a choice—to do things either from love or from fear.
- To master your Mean Girl you must choose love over fear in every moment.
- In times of uncertainty ask yourself, "What would love do right now?"
- You can always light up the darkness of fear with love.

Soul Share

Choose only love. In every moment.
In every circumstance.

TWO

flex your self-love muscle

The most powerful relationship you will ever
have is the relationship with yourself.

STEVE MARABOLI

If the secret to life is choosing love over fear, the keystone of this whole practice is choosing to love *yourself*. Before we go any further, this isn't about being selfish or self-indulgent; it's about honoring yourself wholeheartedly—quirks and all. In fact, the way you feel about yourself is so important, it has an impact on every area of your life—including your health, wealth, and love. That's why flexing your self-love muscle is the next step in mastering your Mean Girl.

You go to the gym to work on your biceps, triceps, and glutes, and the same principle applies for your self-love muscle: it needs to be worked on regularly. You can't just magically expect to have bulging biceps, toned triceps, and firm glutes if you don't do the work. Self-love is exactly the same. A glowing sense of self-esteem and kick-arse self-confidence come only from putting in the work and making it happen.

So let's do it, sister!

Self-Love Is about Cultivation

Before I hit rock bottom, I had a horrible relationship with myself. I loathed my body, the way I looked, the way I felt, and everything about me. Although on the outside I looked like I had my life together, on the inside I was dying. It was not a fun place to be in.

When I was little I remember people saying, "You have to be your own best friend." To be honest, I thought that was a load of BS. Inside, I thought, *I don't have to be my* own *best friend—I already have four best friends at school, and they're awesome!* But of course, they were right. You really do have to be your own bestie if you want to master your Mean Girl and live the life of your dreams.

But if you've spent your whole life thinking that you completely suck, how on earth do you change your own mind?

"I love and accept myself wholeheartedly and unconditionally."

Years ago there was no way I could say that statement aloud, let alone believe it. How many people do you think can truly say they live by such a statement? Not many. Yet if you only knew how truly magnificent you are, you would be treating yourself very differently. The truth is, you are a divine creation of the Universe, and your uniqueness is your special gift you give to the world. Now, it's all well and good for me to tell you this, but *you* have to believe it. You have to really *feel* it with every cell in your entire body and you have to know deep down at your very core just how truly amazing you really are. Merely saying the words isn't enough.

Unfortunately, there's a little hiccup on the way to believing the truth about yourself. You guessed it: your Mean Girl.

I hate to be the bearer of bad news, but that is precisely your Mean Girl's job. She latches onto the experiences you've had in life and uses them against you. She pushes on your sore spots to keep you stuck in Fear Town, especially when it matters the most. She doesn't want you to shine, to choose love, or to be present. Why? Because then she can't run the show. Your Mean Girl cannot survive in the presence of love (which is why learning to flex your self-love muscle is so important!). And remember, it's all about being aware of her voice, gently closing the door on her, and choosing love instead.

When I landed in the hospital and started looking closely at my life, I realized that not only did I have no self-love, I also had no idea how to get it. What I could plainly see, however, was that the way I was treating myself didn't resemble love in the slightest. I was letting my Mean Girl speak to me poorly and call me the most awful names, I was polluting my body, and I had no idea how to go about nurturing myself. However, little by little I started doing things that made me *feel* good and I stopped doing the things that made me contract and feel small. When in doubt, this is the first place you need to start.

Self-Love Exercise

Write down all the things you're doing in your life that make you *feel* small, yucky, contracted, or not in your truth.

_____

_____

_____

_____

_____

Before I hit rock bottom, for me it would have been things like flogging my body at the gym, eating processed low-fat foods, people pleasing, my job, and some of my relationships.

Now write down all the things that make you *feel* light, expansive, "in flow," and aligned with your truth.

_____

_____

_____

_____

For me, these are things like spending time in nature, reading a good book on my balcony, laughing with my boys, conversations with my soul sisters, inspiring women to live their wildest dreams, and watching a sunrise or sunset. These things seriously light me up from my core.

Now that you have these two lists in front of you, I invite you to stop (or at least limit) doing things on the first list and start doing more on the second list, pronto! Life's short, sister! There's no time for things that don't make you feel good and light you up.

The Magic of the Now Moment

After reading Eckhart Tolle's book *The Power of Now*, it was perfectly highlighted to me that we are here on this earth for only a short period of time. What we do every second of every minute of every day matters and is shaping how our life unfolds.

Of course, what happened in the past—even just one minute ago—no longer matters. The past is just a story we keep telling ourselves; it doesn't actually exist anymore. Neither does the future—what's happening in an hour, tomorrow, or next year is just a figment of our imagination. What matters is *this* precious moment right now. *This* second. That's all!

When you realize you don't have to stress out over what happened in the past, and that the future doesn't exist yet, you are left with this beautiful, expansive space in the middle, where infinite possibilities are at your fingertips. How exciting! *This* is where the magic lies, right here in *this* moment . . .

Everyone's path is different (and they must walk it at their own pace).

When we've got experience in a certain area, it's only natural to want to share our wisdom and help the people around us. But of course, this usually has the opposite result from what we intend. The problem is, no one likes to be preached to or told what to do. As soon as we are told we "should" do something, our inner toddler stamps her foot, digs in her heels, and walks staunchly in the opposite direction. I often hear my tribe and clients talk about this phenomenon in frustration: they so badly want to help their partner, their parents, or their bestie, and they feel like they're beating their heads against a brick wall trying to help them or "fix" them. No matter how much they preach, poke, and prod, nothing seems to work. They just find themselves completely exhausted—and sometimes even alienate their loved one in the process.

I remember when I first started on my path to wellness, I was so excited about all the health and wellness information I was learning that I wanted everyone (especially my family) to jump on board. I would lecture my parents about everything they put into their mouths and every lifestyle choice they made. I would shove quinoa down their throats (not literally); I'd try to make them drink green juice, practice yoga, oil pull, do dry body brushing; and I even tried to get them to do coffee enemas. I'm sure you can imagine how that all went down. Not only did they think I was one of the most annoying humans on the planet, they no longer wanted to be around me. It took my parents sitting me down and giving me a tough-love talking-to for me to really pull my head in. I realized in that moment that all I have to do is be the example. Now my mum will call me and tell me about the new cast-iron cookware she bought, the delicious coconut-roasted veggies she just pulled out of the oven, or how amazing her kale chips tasted the first time she made them for her and Dad. And my heart melts when Dad tells me my meditations have allowed him to release stress and are helping him sleep better.

So how do we inspire our loved ones to grow and evolve without barking at them?

Here's the thing we all need to realize: *When it comes to our clients, customers, and loved ones, trying to jam our wisdom in their faces isn't going to work.* We have to take a different approach. One where softness replaces sternness, where "walking our walk" is more important than "talking our talk," and where we lead with our hearts, not our heads.

Here are three beautiful ways to lead with your heart and help the people around you . . .

1. *Be the example.*

We humans learn best by following. Just as a child mimics his parents, we do the same as adults. So when you choose to focus on *inspiring* people and leading by example, they are a million times more likely to follow you than if you simply boss and lecture them. The biggest thing to remember is that in order to inspire someone, you have to genuinely walk your talk and live your message.

The best way to inspire someone is by being the living, breathing example.

But what if you can see someone you love suffering? Is it okay to tell her what to do then? I know it's hard to sit back and let that person go on her own journey—especially when you can see the bigger picture—but the reality is, we cannot save another. Sure, we can *inspire* them, but we cannot *save* them. *You* have to be the example—the shining light that inspires that other person into their brilliance. That's all you can do!

This is a toughie for the parents out there because we so desperately want to save and rescue our children when they are in need. I see it all the time. But by doing that you are actually doing them a disservice. Yep, it may sound counterintuitive but it's true: every time you stop someone else from going through whatever it is they need to go through, you are interfering with their soul lesson and growth process and not allowing them to have a true experience.

I do understand that it's not always easy. Just recently, I could see a very good friend of mine suffering. It broke my heart to see her in pain, but I knew deep down that all I could do was be the light for her, be the example. I let her know that I loved her and was there for her when she needed me, but I did not interrupt her healing process. A few weeks later, when she was ready, she did reach out. Vulnerable, raw, and so beautiful. She thanked me for holding space for her and was grateful she got so much growth out of that particular experience. Remember, all you can do is be the light. Be that beautiful, shiny beacon ahead for your clients, team, or loved ones.

2. *Let them know that you are one hundred percent there for them.*

When we are processing something, we can feel extremely isolated. So simply letting your loved one know you are truly there for them can be incredibly powerful. Sometimes they might not want to hear it, but keep letting them know that you are there whenever they need you. I do this by sending text messages, Soul Shares, or "just thinking of you" e-mails or by simply sending them love at the end of my meditation. You don't want to be too over-the-top with this—know your limits and don't be annoying. Use your intuition and gauge when enough is enough.

3. *Stay soft.*

I know it can sometimes feel heart wrenching and frustrating watching someone struggling, but the last thing they need is you nagging. Stay soft, grounded, and anchored in your heart—they are more likely going to turn to you when you are in your heart space.

Also, remember that "when the student is ready, the teacher appears." I strongly felt like this when I first started meditating. I wanted to teach everyone how to meditate, but after exhausting myself (and getting nowhere), I remembered that on my own journey, I had to reach a state of readiness within myself before I was able to make a change. Then, once I *was* ready, the teachers and wisdom I needed seemed to appear as if by magic. Remember this when it comes to your loved ones—when they are ready, the Universe will send them what they need.

Soul Share

Your actions speak louder than your words.
Be the example, don't just speak it.

The Great Expectations

Expectation (noun): an attitude of expectancy or hope, anticipation.

Expectations are one of the biggest killers of self-love and relationships, a fact I know all too well. Here's a sample of some of the expectations that used to play over and over again on my mental mixtape:

- I will love and accept you, Melissa ... when you get rid of your cellulite.
- I will love and accept you, Melissa ... when you get that high-paying TV gig.
- I will love and accept you, Melissa ... when you're out of debt.
- I will love and accept you, Melissa ... when you've found your soul mate.
- I will love and accept you, Melissa ... when you buy your own home.
- I will love and accept you, Melissa ... when you can run the next city marathon.
- I will love and accept you, Melissa ... when you have perfectly glowing skin.

Sound familiar?

These sorts of expectations are oh so common to women; I know I subscribed to them myself for a long time. They are your Mean Girl's way of keeping you in the penthouse in Fear Town—and, damn, she does a good job of it! When you see them written down like this, however, you realize just how ridiculous they are.

I also used to place a boatload of expectations on the people around me, and let me tell you one thing ... *Expectations are the fastest way to ruin relationships.*

For example, I thought that just because my mum was my mum, she should do certain things for me and put up with me sometimes speaking to her poorly. I thought that just because my boyfriend was my partner, I could speak to him horribly and he should take it and still love me. I thought that because people were my friends, they should be there to pick up my phone calls, rush to my rescue, and make sure I was always okay. Instead of allowing each of these people to show up exactly how they were, I would be disappointed when they didn't match *my* ideas and the expectations I'd placed on them. *How dare they not meet my expectations?* What a crazy and totally self-indulgent way to live.

Whenever you have expectations, you will always be disappointed.

Instead of expecting your partner to do the dishes, simply communicate lovingly and openly that you would like some help in the kitchen. Instead of expecting your children to behave well in the car, simply communicate from a place of love. Expectations fester inside us, slowly eating away at our soul.

Let go of your expectations, open your heart, stay connected to your truth, and simply communicate your desires from your heart to others and yourself.

I do understand how tough it can be to let go of them sometimes. One year for my birthday, I placed a big fat expectation on one of my friends: I expected her to call and wish me happy birthday. After all, I reasoned, isn't that what friends do? When she didn't I got very upset and angry. I held on to that anger for weeks, letting it fester away inside me. I lost sleep over it and couldn't understand what I had done wrong. I was too stubborn to confront her about it, so I let it eat away at me until she finally came to me and shared what had been going on for her. She was dealing with some very heavy family stuff and apologized profusely for forgetting my birthday. I felt so silly for carrying that anger and resentment around for weeks over something so small when all I had to do was drop my expectations and allow her to show up however was perfect for her.

When you drop your expectations—of both yourself and others—you open yourself up to infinite possibilities. You allow the energy to flow freely and more effortlessly, and spontaneity can move through you. But when you are high and mighty with your expectations, you build a dam that blocks that life-force.

This principle plays out so often in our daily lives, often without us even being aware of it. For example, on one occasion, I was picking up Leo from school, a task I love doing. I was excited to see him, as usual. We were going to head to the beach to throw around the Frisbee, kick the soccer ball, and have a swim—some of our favorite things to do. As soon as he got in the car I could tell something was up. He was cranky and emotional. He snapped at me, and my sunglasses began to fog up and tears started to stream down my cheeks. I sucked it up to be "strong," something I had learned watching my parents growing up. It was weak to show emotions, right? This was something that later in life I had to unlearn.

But this incident triggered me so much that I defaulted back into an old pattern.

Despite feeling a little sad in my heart we still had our play at the beach, but when we got home I pondered why I had been so affected by his actions. I realized it was because I had expectations of how this divine little boy "should" show up for me. What I had "future-tripped" (that is, mapped out in my mind) was "supposed" to happen was this: I'd pick him up from school, he'd run up to me with a massive smile on his face and leap into my arms, we'd kiss each other's faces off, and then we'd head to the beach. *Warning . . . expectation overload!* I had no idea what had gone on for him that day at school. Maybe someone was nasty, maybe he fell over and hurt himself, or maybe he was just hot and cranky and needed a minute to settle down after school. But because I showed up with expectations of how *I* wanted *him* to show up, I was left disappointed. My expectations took me out of the present moment with him at the beach and blocked me from being wholeheartedly available, present, and open.

This principle applies just as much to your romantic relationships. I have a beautiful relationship with my husband and this is the first relationship I have been in where I have no expectations of my partner. I want Nick to just be himself. When I allow him the space and freedom to just be his true self, he shows up as the best version of him. No expectations needed. Having a mile-long running list of expectations is going to do nothing but ruin our relationship. Let go of your expectations and be open to whatever magic is coming your way.

Inspo-action

Write down all the expectations you've placed on your-self right now—whether it's to do with your body, your work, your relationship, or whatever.

_____

_____

_____

_____

_____

Now read them back to yourself. For each one, ask yourself if you'd place those expectations on your best friend. Likely answer? Hell no! So don't place them on yourself, beautiful. Loosen your Mean Girl's grip on you by letting go of your own expectations.

Letting go of your expectations on yourself and others will free you and allow you to live your best life.

Expectations are a field day for your Mean Girl. Refuse to play her games. Simply release them and show up present and as the most authentic you. Always remember that if you don't have expectations, you can never be disappointed. It's also a good indicator that if you have expectations you aren't practicing presence. _Expectations ruin relationships._ So let go of them and allow yourself (and everyone else) to show up exactly the way they are meant to—then you are allowing yourself to have a true experience.

Self-Love Is Not Selfish

To love oneself is the beginning of a lifelong romance.
OSCAR WILDE

Let's get one thing straight: self-love is not selfish. Self-love is the cornerstone of happiness. However, it's a concept that women really struggle with. But let me break this down for you: in order for you to be the best, happiest, shiniest version of yourself, you need to fill *yourself* up first so that you are overflowing and bursting with love. If you aren't flexing your self-love muscle and looking after yourself, you will show up to the world as a cranky, half-arsed version of yourself. Do you want to show up as a cranky wife, mother, sister, daughter, colleague, or boss? Hell no! I personally want to show up every single day to the world as the full-blissed version of me—the best wife, stepmama, sister, daughter, boss, teacher, and soul sister I can be. In order to do this, I have to look after myself and flex *my* self-love muscle every single day.

I can hear you mamas out there saying, "But, Melissa, I have four children under the age of nine and can't even steal five minutes by myself to pee in peace!" I hear you, sister! However, just like on an airplane, you have to put on your own oxygen mask before you help the person next to you. You are no good to anyone (even your kids) if you aren't the full bursting-with-love you. I know this can be a hard concept to grasp, but bear with me. Try it out for a week and see how you feel. Give your kiddies a task: maybe a book that makes farm noises, a puzzle with giant pieces that they can't put in their mouth, or some Duplo. Don't give them paint or Play-Doh; give them something that will entertain them safely so you don't have to worry they will paint the couch blue, like my nephew once did, or think the playdough is their dinner. All it takes is five minutes alone with a cuppa and maybe even the sunshine on your face. Commit to that for one single week and feel the difference.

Many years ago this concept was a hard one for me to grasp. I grew up watching all the women in my life—especially my mother and nonna—put everyone else before themselves. (In fact, they still do.) My mother is amazing, one of the most giving, nurturing, and loving people I know. I remember whenever a family member or friend or even the woman who lived down the street was unwell, she would make them lasagne (from scratch) or her beautiful crumbed chicken. My mum is a nurse and midwife, so she naturally has that caring nature about her, but she doesn't know how to fill herself up, always putting herself at the bottom of her to-do list.

When I was growing up she worked night duty so she could take my sister, brother, and me to school. She would work all night from ten p.m. till six a.m., get home, iron our uniforms, make our lunches, then do the school drop-off (to three different schools, I might add). She would come home and sleep from around nine a.m. till two thirty p.m., then it was back in the car to pick us all up and drop my sister to tutoring, me to dancing, and my brother to rugby practice. Most times she would sleep in the car while I was in dance class because she was too tired to drive home and then come back out again. Bless her. After our activities, it was home for a beautiful meal she had somehow found the time to prepare, followed by homework, then bed. If she was lucky she could sneak in a few more hours of sleep on the couch from seven thirty p.m. till nine p.m., before it was time to head to work again.

I remember how exhausted she always was. I remember her falling asleep at every opportunity she got. Sometimes she would even doze off for a minute or two when we were stopped at the traffic lights on the way home from dancing: she would get me to wake her when the light turned green.

Back then, I thought that was just what mums did—sacrificed themselves for their children. But this is not the way *I* want to live my life, and I'm guessing it's not how you want to live yours either. I am so incredibly grateful for what Mum did, but we don't have to live like that.

I have also seen way too many cases with my clients where they put their children first their whole lives—actually their children *are* their entire world, so when the kids finally move out of the home, the mums feel like their life has lost all meaning. The void manifests as an illness or a classic midlife crisis. We don't have to live like *that* either. Just because you choose to fill yourself up and address your own needs doesn't mean you love your children any less. It actually means quite the opposite. It means you love your children so much that you want to be fully present and bursting with love when you're with them and give them the absolute best version of yourself. Because that is what they deserve.

Here's a good way to think of it: Imagine a mug of water sitting on a saucer. The mug is overflowing with water and it's pouring out onto the saucer. Because the mug is overflowing, you have extra water in the saucer to give freely to others. But if your mug were only half full, you wouldn't have much to share around. Let's make sure we are overflowing with love first so that we can give from that overflowing place of love.

Soul Share

Fill yourself up first and give from the overflow.
It is only then you can truly give.

With regard to Leo, I need to make sure I am bursting with love so that I can show up fully for him. When he's with us it doesn't mean I stop meditating, doing yoga, or all the other things that light me up. He doesn't deserve tired, cranky Melissa; he deserves vibrant, bursting-with-love Melissa. Same goes for everyone else. But I know we mamas think it's incredibly selfish to sit and take a few deep belly breaths to calm and ground ourselves. *How dare we take ten minutes—our kids need us!* This is a load of BS, and the sooner you get over it, the sooner you can master your Mean Girl. You can practice mindfulness, meditate, and ground yourself when you're sitting on the loo, when the kids are sleeping, or while you're standing in the line at the post office or stopped at traffic lights. It's okay to take ten minutes, or simply three mindful breaths, to bring you back to your center: your kids will be okay. Go and take that time to breathe, meditate, have an Epsom salt bath, ground your feet in the grass, or have that cuppa in the sun. Whatever it is that lights you up and makes you feel most you, *do it!*

If you don't take time out for yourself, you're doing yourself and everyone around you a disservice.

Remember, you can only truly serve from the overflow.

One of my clients, Sarah, has three kids and is a stay-at-home mum. Two of the kiddies are in school and the other is two years old. When she first started coaching with me, she was exhausted, looked like she'd had a fight with the hair dryer, and was on the brink of a nervous breakdown. We threw around some suggestions for arranging child care for her youngest for a few hours a week so she could use that time for herself. Sarah and her family had just moved away from all their family and friends, so getting someone close and trusted to babysit was out of the question, and her partner needed to work full-time to support their family, so the only option was putting her bub in a playgroup down the road for half a day each week. She burst into tears and said, "Oh no, Melissa, I could *never* do that. I don't work and it would make me such a horrible mother!" I explained to her the concept of self-love and that she needed to fill herself up in order to be the best mother to her children.

A few weeks later at our next session, she looked like a completely different person—the bags had gone from under her eyes, her hair was combed and clean, and she had a glow about her. She said, "Melissa, I did it. I got some extra help one day a week! I feel so much better and so much more *me*." She informed me that she cried the first day she wasn't with her little bub for the whole day, but having the space for herself had done her a world of good. She also realized that she had placed expectations on herself of what a stay-at-home mother "should" look and be like. With the extra time and space, she was able to get on top of the housework, the bills, and the general life admin that we all have. She's now more present when she's with the kids and doesn't resent not having any time and space for herself and her dreams. After a few weeks of having that space she began to explore her passions and is considering starting an online business. That would not have happened if she hadn't created that space in her life—you *need* space for magic to flow through.

But please know I really do get it—you want to be with your children or partner all the time. I don't blame you: me too! But wouldn't you rather be with your kids or partner ninety percent of the time and be bursting with love, patience, and presence? Or would you rather be with them one hundred percent of the time, wanting to rip your own hair out? The choice is yours, my love. I know which one I choose.

Being busy doesn't mean you stop looking after yourself. It means you fill yourself up even more so you can show up as the best version of you.

Stop the Glorification of Busy

Does this dialogue sound familiar?

> *"Hey! How are you?"*
> *"Busy, as usual. Yourself?"*
> *"Yeah—really busy. Life's just crazy, you know?"*
> *"Yep, I totally get it. It's crazy busy."*

We live in a world where it's not only cool to be busy: it's glorified. It's the first thing we say when we greet each other. You're given a pat on the back when you pull a hefty thirteen-hour day or an all-nighter or if you've rushed around like a mad thing to meet a deadline. We wear our busyness like a badge of honor and will proudly tell everyone in our lives how crazy and hectic things are.

For me, there's nothing glamorous or sexy about "being busy." In fact, it's something I want to steer away from. I don't want to be run off my feet, stressed out, and overwhelmed. Instead, I choose to move through my day with ease and grace. How much nicer does that sound?

While we're busting through myths and misconceptions, let's debunk another one: life isn't about trying to find "balance" either. I think the idea of striving for balance is unrealistic . . . and kind of destructive. Besides, it doesn't even exist—it's just another thing women use to compare ourselves with one another. We even use it as a self-inflicted weapon to make ourselves feel guilty and unworthy. *I spent way too much time at work this week; I'm such a bad mama. I didn't tick everything off my to-do list today; I'm such a failure.* (Can you believe the awful things our Mean Girl says to us sometimes?)

The fact is there are times when my work requires more of me. Like when I'm hunkering down to write this book or I'm knee-deep in a speaking tour or launching a new online product or program. There are also times when my family or friends need me more, and everything else gets put to the side so I can show up fully for them. I believe it's all about being present and riding the waves of life. Sometimes one particular area will call for more energy and more love and it's our job to be so aware and tuned in that we can recognize it and act accordingly. It's all about being adaptable and less rigid.

*Instead of rigidly striving for "balance," tune in to the natural
ebbs and flows of life—that's where the magic is.*

Ready to take action?

If you want to ditch the feeling of being overwhelmed and avoid
the busyness trap once and for all (and supercharge your productivity while you're at it), try these seven hot tips:

1. *Start using your calendar (preferably a digital calendar).*

   I used to love using a pretty handheld calendar that I would
   carry around in my handbag everywhere I went. But not only
   was it chunky and extremely heavy, I also found myself missing appointments and stuffing up times because the inside of
   my planner looked like my two-year-old nephew had taken to
   the pages with a bunch of pens! We live in a fast-paced world
   where things move and change all the time, and constantly
   crossing out and writing over things takes time and can look
   overwhelming (especially if you have handwriting like mine!).
   It's so easy to move things around on your digital calendar.
   Plus you can sync it to your smartphone and computer, which
   makes booking things in very convenient. You can also send
   calendar invites to other people so they don't miss your meeting or catch up. And the best part is you can share your calendar with your family members, making it super easy to
   know what's on and when.

2. *Make sure you schedule in time for you.*

   I know I've said it before and I know it feels ridiculous that
   we have to actually schedule in downtime, but we do: if we

don't, it doesn't happen! I personally make sure my yoga, meditation, and afternoon self-love hour are all added to my digital calendar; otherwise, I know they'll just fall by the wayside. Set yourself up for success by scheduling in your self-love time today. You can also make it a recurring task, which saves you time and makes sure these essential activities are always front and center in your day.

3. *Delegate.*

For many years, I really struggled with this. My business is my baby, so handing anything over to someone else scared the bejesus out of me. But since I learned to delegate, I have really been able to focus my attention on what I love and am best at, which is writing, speaking, teaching, sharing, and creating. As a result, my business has grown exponentially.

To make this shift for yourself, work out what *you* love doing in your business or job. If you love writing and creating content, and don't necessarily love sending invoices, bookkeeping, and assigning tags in Infusionsoft (also lovingly known among team MA as Confusionsoft), then hire someone else to do it. You need to stay in your zone of genius and stop wasting your precious time doing things you don't enjoy. Life's too short to do anything that doesn't light you up.

4. *Ask for help.*

There's a common misconception that we have to do it all alone and that if we don't, we're a failure. This is BS. When you really let go of that belief—and simply ask for help when you need it—you can avoid burnout and stop "overwhelm" in its tracks. Give it a go.

Asking for help isn't an act of weakness; it's an act of self-love.

5. *Do the brain dump.*

Things, which is a management app, is one of my favorite productivity tools. Every morning I do a brain dump into the app, which helps stop my brain from swirling into overwhelm mode and falling into that unproductive busyness trap.

6. *Meditate.*

Want to supercharge your productivity? Meditate! But let me guess: you're too busy and don't have time, right? Wrong. We all have the same amount of hours in the day, though of course we all have varying degrees of full-ness—it's about prioritizing yourself, scheduling it in your calendar, then showing up every single day.

7. *Eat your frog first.*

Once you get all your tasks out of your head and into the Things app either on your phone or computer, you need to start organizing them. Divide your brain dump into four categories:

- Tasks you don't like, but that are important (the frogs).
- Tasks you like, and that are important.
- Tasks you like, but that are unimportant.

- Tasks you don't like, and that are unimportant (these can sneak in there).

Once you've got your list organized, it's time to prioritize the sections. The most important place to start? The "frogs." These are the things you don't enjoy, but that actually really need to be done. They're the ones you aren't motivated to do and that send you spiraling into procrastination. In fact, they can hang over your head all day and fill you with guilt . . . yet you still can't bring yourself to actually get them done.

So how do we tackle our frogs? Frogs need structure around them to ensure that they actually get finished. You can create the motivation you need to make them happen by either transforming them into something desirable (say, turning your weekly vacuuming session into a lounge-room dance jam) or building a pleasant routine around them (say, doing admin and invoicing while sitting in the sun with a cuppa and your favorite tunes playing in the background).

In his book *Eat That Frog!*, Brian Tracy suggests that the best habit to get into is eating your frogs first thing in the morning, which is exactly how I like to structure my to-do list. Not only does it mean you get the icky stuff over with first (leaving you free to do the things you enjoy without a cloud of guilt hanging over your head), but it's also incredibly rewarding. Within the first hour or so of my workday, I already feel like I've made great headway, and that surge of momentum helps me glide through the rest of my day with ease and grace. (Like Mark Twain once said, if you have to eat a live frog, it does not pay to sit and look at it for a very long time!)

BONUS TIP: BAN THE B WORD

My team and I have also eliminated the word "busy" from our vocabulary. It helps a lot! Try it if you like. And next time someone asks you how you are, try not to respond with, "Oh, I am so busy." Instead, connect with how you're actually feeling and go from there.

AND A SPECIAL NOTE FOR THE MAMAS . . .

So many women struggle with taking time for themselves—especially mothers. Society has conditioned us to believe that we "should" be able to do it all without any help, and if we don't, then we are, well, a failure. But if you take a look at different cultures around the world, motherhood is a whole lot different. Elsewhere mums are often surrounded by a large support network of their parents, grandparents, brothers, sisters, uncles, aunts, friends, and community—there are whole villages and tribes that help raise the children. Yet in the West there's an expectation that mothers should do it all alone.

Free yourself from this social conditioning and fill yourself up with self-love and get ready to start giving from your overflow. I also understand that not everyone has family or a network around them, and at times you may feel incredibly lonely—maybe you have lost your partner or just moved and know absolutely no one in your new town—but even in that case there are so many things you can do. Think about joining online parenting group forums in your area; go to your local community center and read the notice board for groups that inspire you and could support you and your interests; head out and meet your neighbors; start chatting with the other parents at school and see whether you could start a meal swap, where you all make a large amount of one meal and swap it with the other parents to save you cooking every night. You could also swap babysitting, so you can alternate having a few hours at night for yourself, or start a carpooling roster with a few other parents. The options are infinite and limited only by your imagination. Get creative and think of ways that are going to best serve you and your needs.

If you're waiting for permission—as Sarah was—for someone to say, "It's okay to take time for yourself," then I am granting you that permission right now.

Self-Love Permission Slip

Name:

Date:

What is this permission slip for? To flex your self-love muscle daily.

When for? For the rest of your life.

Where does this take place? Right now in this present moment.

Why is it happening? Because life is short and you are amazing.

What you need: An open heart.

I, Melissa Ambrosini, give _____ full permission to flex her self-love muscle and do things like get a blow-dry, do some yoga in her lounge room, meditate, or sip herbal tea in the garden with her bestie on a daily basis. I allow her to do things that light her up and that are her truth from this day forward.

Melissa Ambrosini

Head to my website to download your free permission slip. Print it out and stick it somewhere prominent so you can always be reminded that you are allowed to fill yourself up.

Making It Happen

So now we know that self-love is essential, and that it's definitely not selfish, how do we actually create more of it in our lives? Ultimately, you want to be choosing love over fear in every single moment; however, the self-love tools outlined on the following pages are going to help you become a love magnet.

Magical Meditation

From my early teens I suffered from serious anxiety and panic attacks. I remember my first attack like it was yesterday. I wasn't really interested in school until I hit year eleven, when I realized that I may as well make the most of my last two years, and so I knuckled down and put in the work. I got great grades as a result but often got quite stressed out in the process. One time, I was putting the final touches on a huge assignment. It was for an English essay I had worked hard on all term, and I was super proud of it. As I was saving the last few changes on my chunky old-school desktop computer, the floppy disk—for those of you youngsters who don't know what that is, Google it!—decided to break down and corrupt, wiping my whole assignment. For some odd reason I didn't have it saved anywhere else, so my entire assignment was gone. Fear, panic, anger, sadness, and frustration washed over me like a tsunami. I started hyperventilating and sweating and I couldn't breathe; I felt like I was dying. Tears streaming down my cheeks and short of breath, I punched the air like a four-year-old child having a tantrum. This went on for a while. I'm sure my parents thought I was crazy, but when you are in a panic attack it feels entirely real, like there is no escape. For those hectic few minutes, I truly thought my world was coming to an end.

From then on, this kind of thing happened quite regularly. Whenever something was out of my control or didn't go my way, I would have an attack. It began to affect other areas of my life, particularly my sleeping. I would lie awake at night stressing over schoolwork or something someone had said to me that day. So at age sixteen, I was prescribed and began taking sleeping pills. This was a very bad habit to get into because I then became dependent on them. This continued for years and it wasn't until I started meditating in my early twenties that things began to get better. Meditation was like a magic tonic for my panic-stricken mind. My anxiety, panic attacks, and depression dissipated, and I also began to sleep better and feel more vital. These are just a handful of the incredible benefits meditation has had on my life—enough to make me a lifelong convert.

Meditation's power lies in its ability to help us notice—and ultimately quieten—the endless Mean Girl chatter that goes on in our minds. Often we get so used to this background noise that we're not even aware of it anymore, which creates the perfect conditions for our Mean Girl to take over. It is this fear-based mental chatter that for some people can be the greatest source of stress in their lives.

Thankfully, meditation is one of the simplest tools to still your mind, master your Mean Girl, and bring you back to present-moment awareness. Once awareness rises, so does wisdom, and the wisdom and creativity that come from meditation are extremely powerful and transformational.

Meditation brings you back to the present moment and is a breeding ground for miracles.

Meditation is one of Mother Nature's most powerful medicines and has no apparent side effects. It's been scientifically proven that meditation helps calm the mind and de-stress the body. It also helps regulate blood pressure, lowers depression, induces the "relaxation response," rewires the circuitry of your brain, enhances positive emotions, and increases overall life satisfaction . . . And that's just for starters!

This ancient practice has been around for more than five thousand years. Some of the most enlightened beings to walk this planet meditated, like the Buddha, Krishna, and Jesus. Although many of their teachings have been layered in dogma, there is one thing that binds them together: meditation.

Make no mistake: it's the fastest, easiest, and cheapest way to master your Mean Girl and flex your self-love muscle. There is no pill, potion, quick fix, or supplement that can create this type of internal alchemy; it's truly in a class of its own.

But there's a reason why so many people don't do it. It takes dedication, commitment, and persistence! You have to regularly commit to sitting yourself down, gently closing the door on your Mean Girl, and focusing on your breath or your mantra. This is the work we need to do in order to cultivate beautiful relationships with ourselves and to master our Mean Girls. And I will be the first to admit that sometimes it's not easy.

I meditate for twenty minutes twice a day—more if I am not feeling well, if I'm flying, or if I have a fuller schedule than usual. Since I committed to this practice I have noticed many changes. I am calmer, more grounded, less stressed, and generally a lot nicer to be around (a mega bonus!).

This sort of commitment takes discipline and courage. You can't let your Mean Girl give you a million excuses as to why you shouldn't meditate. The e-mails can wait, the to-do list will still be there when you're done, and the house will get cleaned. Everything in divine time. Nothing is more important than turning inward and connecting with your true essence. That is where the magic lies. That is the magical spot that oozes sweet nectar. That is where the miracles occur and the manifestation begins. Regularly tapping into it will lead you down the path of bliss. There is no other answer. Meditation is key!

Inspo-action

It's time to start right now. Here's a simple meditation.

1. Find somewhere quiet where you won't be disturbed. Turn off your phone and remove any distractions.

2. Sit upright in a chair or cross-legged on the floor with your lower back supported. Make sure you are comfortable. Your spine should be straight, your chin slightly tucked in, and your eyes and lips gently closed.

3. Relax your shoulders and take a deep breath in through your nose for four counts, hold for two counts, and slowly release the air out through your nose for four counts. Focus all your attention on your breath. Whenever your mind starts to wander, gently bring it back to your breath and keep going. Continue this for five to ten minutes.

That's it—you're meditating!

This is an ancient Indian technique called *pranayama*. It's incredibly powerful and something I use daily. Start by aiming for just five to ten minutes each day, and slowly increase to twenty minutes or longer.

If you want to try one of my guided meditations, head to my website and download your free manifestation meditation to really amp things up.

It's important to note that thoughts are part of meditation. So if thoughts keep popping up, great! Simply observe them, allow them to be there, then let them go. Don't think you can't meditate or that you're not doing it right; you're doing just fine. Thoughts are part of the process. The difference between a newbie meditator and a seasoned pro is that the seasoned pro notices the thoughts pop up and simply releases them. The pro doesn't engage with them and run off with the story. For the new kid on the block, a thought might pop up, which will then ignite a feeling, which leads to the person running off with the story and down the rabbit hole of mental Mean Girl chatter. The trick is that when thoughts pop up (and they will), don't engage with them; gently let them go and bring your attention back to the present moment by focusing on your breath.

It's important to have fun with meditation and don't take it too seriously. With commitment to yourself, it can become the most rewarding part of your day. I actually look forward to my sessions and can't wait to dive into that peaceful, blissed-out space.

All the girls in the MA office practice meditation. Toward the end of our workday we stop, drop, and meditate. It's a beautiful ritual we all love and look forward to. And for my morning sesh, I meditate with Nick, usually while Leo is eating breakfast and getting dressed for school. It's nonnegotiable.

It's also great to get your kids involved. From the age of five, children can learn Transcendental Meditation (which is what I practice). Leo learned at that age and we always invite him to join us for a medi. Sometimes he does and other times he doesn't. It's important to always invite your children to join you, but never pressure them.

You will find that they naturally will be more inclined the younger you introduce them to it. You can also listen to guided meditations with them, which is great to do just before bed. Leo listens to a twenty-minute guided meditation every night before bed. It helps calm the parasympathetic nervous system and promotes a deeper, more healing sleep. He used to wake up during the night and, since introducing his twenty-minute meditation, he no longer wakes up. You can really tell the difference with children who meditate. They have a presence, calmness, and groundedness about them. And remember, others (especially your children) learn most by following what you do, so lead by example. If you show up every single day to your meditation pillow they will be inspired by that and eventually want to try it out. Be persistent and consistent!

QUIT WITH THE EXCUSES

Your Mean Girl is going to try to find a million and one excuses why you shouldn't meditate. As my meditation teacher Tom Cronin says, we have seventy-two lots of twenty-minute blocks in our day. If you allocate only two of those for meditation, you still have seventy for everything else. And those seventy will be a lot more productive if you use two of them to meditate.

Tom also says that one twenty-minute meditation is the equivalent of four hours' sleep. So on average, if you're meditating twice a day for twenty minutes you are in fact getting an extra eight hours' sleep each day. Sign me up for that in a heartbeat!

Get Grateful

Gratitude is a powerful force. When you are grateful, you become a laser-charged magnet for more things to be grateful for. At the moment I have five types of gratitude practices I perform daily.

As soon as I wake up in the morning I roll over, kiss my husband, and ask, "What are three things you are grateful for?" He shares his, then I share mine.

Each day at the end of my meditation, I sit in stillness—eyes closed, hands in prayer—and consciously and deliberately feel everything and everyone I am grateful for.

When I sit down at my desk to start my workday, a reminder pops up and asks me to write down everything I am grateful for.

When we sit down for dinner each night we hold hands and share how grateful we are for the beautiful, healthy, nourishing food we have in front of us.

As we tuck Leo into bed at night, after the kisses and cuddles, we each share one thing we are grateful for from the day.

As I sit here and share this with you I realize it was never a conscious decision I set out to perform five daily acts of gratitude. It just happened because when I express what I am grateful for it makes me feel good. And I am all about doing things that feel good and not doing things that don't.

These practices are now so important to me that if I miss a day, I can feel it. I feel off. On the days I do it I am lighter and move through my day with a sense of ease and grace.

But why is this?

Being grateful helps you see the good and get perspective on life. It allows you to see the light even when times can feel really dark. For example, it's tough to feel bad about your "flabby" arms when you're grateful for your four working limbs. Or it's difficult to get angry about your children's mess when you are so grateful you have the little munchkins in the first place. Or it's hard to feel annoyed at your boss when you are grateful to have a job to go to.

It reminds you to thank others. Never underestimate the simple act of saying "thank you" to someone who has helped you in some way. We humans love to be acknowledged and appreciated, and your simple act of kindness could really change the course of someone's day.

Bonus: making someone else happy in turn makes you even happier.

It forces you to take stock of all the brilliant things in your life. It's easy to get caught up in lamenting all the things you don't have, rather than noticing the wonderful things you do have. I used to always focus on the fact that I didn't have enough money, I hadn't gotten the gig I wanted, I wasn't living in my dream home, I didn't fit into my jeans, my skin was bad, and I didn't have a soul mate. Constantly focusing on what you don't have energetically emphasizes your lack, giving you a double dose of it. But when you consciously express what you are truly grateful for you are saying a big fat *thank you!* to the Universe and becoming a magnet for more of that goodness to come into your life. It's a win-win.

I definitely haven't always had a grateful heart, or a daily practice, for that matter. Like I mentioned before, my mental mixtape was always full of songs about lack and fear. But after hitting rock bottom and studying some of the happiest and most successful people on the planet, I realized they all had one thing in common: they had some form of gratitude practice embedded in their daily routine.

So when I was in the hospital, I asked my mum to bring me a journal and I started writing down everything I was grateful for.

I am grateful that I have my parents by my side right now.

I am grateful for the doctors who are easing my pain.

I am grateful for hitting rock bottom, because I see that I wasn't treating myself with love and respect.

I am grateful for my friends who sent flowers and teddy bears.

I am grateful that I can now see I was letting my Mean Girl run the show.

Although it was the darkest and most challenging experience I had faced at that point, I was still able to start to shift my mentality from fear to love and adopt an attitude of gratitude. So every day— even when I didn't feel like it—I wrote down what I was grateful for, and, although I was in physical pain and very unhappy, I slowly started to feel lighter.

Soul Share

There can't be joy until there is gratitude.

In order to experience more joy, happiness, and love in your life, you must adopt an attitude of gratitude. My life did not start to flow until I really got serious about gratitude.

Follow these steps to cultivate an elegant gratitude practice.

STEP 1: *Commit, girlfriend.*

Choose a time within your day that is your designated "gratitude time." You can do it first thing in the morning, in the shower, after your meditation, in the car on the school drop-off, at the dinner table, on the bus on the way to work, or just before bed. The nice thing about doing it first thing in the morning, though, is that it sets the tone for the day ahead and sends you out into the world with a full and grateful heart.

STEP 2: *Just do it.*

As with meditation, your Mean Girl will make up hundreds of excuses as to why you can't do it. Surely taking out the rubbish first thing in the morning is more important. Or replying to that e-mail at six a.m. Or sleeping in. Don't listen to her excuses, beautiful; just do it, and do it every single day. Remember, consistency counts.

STEP 3: *Write it down.*

There have been times when I have simply listed what I am grateful for out loud or rattled them off in my head. That's definitely better than nothing, but there is something even more powerful about actually writing it down in your journal. The simple act of putting pen to paper is making an even more potent declaration to the Universe.

Don't have a pen and paper? Type it in the notes app in your phone. I have a gratitude list I keep right there on my home screen, which I always add to if I don't have my journal handy.

STEP 4: *Get a buddy.*

Before I met my husband, a friend and I were each other's "gratitude buddy" for about a year. Every morning we would text each other a list of the things we were grateful for. Sometimes the list was long and sometimes it was short, but it didn't matter. What did matter was being held accountable—knowing someone else was counting on me to get it done. I now do this practice with my husband each morning.

STEP 5: *Keep going.*

When things start to flow, don't get ahead of yourself. Keep showing up every day. A few years ago, when my life (finally!) started to flow and things were looking up, I felt like I had everything under control and I got a little complacent, so I decided to drop my gratitude practice. Within days I felt the gloomy effect of not doing it, so I got straight back into it. The good thing is it never takes long to get into the swing.

The whole idea of a gratitude practice really is quite simple, but don't let its simplicity deceive you. It's a beautiful thing to do with your family, your partner, your team—it's even a great conversation starter at a dinner party. (Imagine your next dinner party: everyone sits down and you each share one thing you are grateful for . . . How beautiful!)

What am I grateful for today?

For you, my beautiful reader, for honoring yourself and taking the first steps to master your Mean Girl.

- For my divine husband and soul mate. I am grateful for all that he stands for and for the fact that I get to share this journey with him. I am honored!

- For Leo and the cuddles I got this morning in bed. And for being the easiest and most divine little monkey ever.

- For my parents for creating me, and my mum for giving birth to me. And for their consistent unconditional love.

- For my dream in-laws. I am so grateful to have them in my life.

- For organic food and all its nourishment.

- For my daily asana of yoga, meditation, and gratitude that allows me to connect with myself.

- For all my teachers, guides, and mentors who have led me back to the truth of who I am.

- For clean water, fresh air, Mother Nature, and all her divinity.

- For my online and offline tribe, who strive to live their best lives every day.

- For my soul sisters and blood brother and sister.

- For my epic team, who I get to create magic with every day.

- For the belly laughs I had with Leo while jumping on the rebounder to One Direction (don't judge me).

I could go on forever, but I will leave that for the gratitude section at the end of this book.

Your gratitude practice doesn't have to be reserved for your home. Every morning at the MA HQ, we go around and each express three things we are grateful for. It's a great way to start the day.

The fact is, the more we express what we are truly grateful for, the more love, joy, and happiness we will cultivate in our lives. It really is that simple.

Inspo-action

Close your eyes, take a few deep breaths, and focus inward. Ask yourself, "What am I deeply grateful for right now?" Take your time to jot it down.

_____

_____

_____

_____

_____

_____

_____

_____

_____

How nice does that feel?!

Getting your whole family involved in this practice is also very powerful. You can do it anytime, anywhere—from the breakfast table to the school pickup, to your night-time snuggle session—but remember: consistency is key. It's the little things we do each day that add up to big results or big consequences.

More Ways to Flex Your Self-Love Muscle

Gratitude and meditation are the two cornerstones of my self-love practice, but there are so many other ways you can flex your self-love muscle and get it in seriously good shape. To round out this chapter, here are some other brilliant ways to shower yourself with love and fall head over heels for the amazingness of you.

1. *Use affirmations.*

   Stand in front of the mirror. Stare into those gorgeous eyes of yours and repeat any of these affirmations:

   - I love and accept myself unconditionally and wholeheartedly, right now!
   - I am perfect exactly the way I am.
   - Joy is my barometer for deep self-love.
   - I inhale love; I exhale fear.
   - I do all things with love.
   - I choose love over fear in every moment.
   - My thoughts create my reality, so I choose only loving thoughts that are going to deeply support and nourish me.
   - I open my heart to love.

   Repeat, repeat, and repeat again. But don't just say the words: really feel them with every fiber of your being. I remember when I first started using affirmations I really struggled. I couldn't even look myself in the eyes without bursting into tears. All I saw was this little girl in pain, who was choosing to suffer. But I pushed through and I am so glad I did. Keep going with it. If feelings or emotions arise, just allow them to wash over you like a wave and stay connected to your heart. Don't run off with the stories; stay present. Be persistent with this and remember that consistency counts.

Affirmations might seem simplistic, but they can be truly powerful. One of my clients, Megan, came to me very unhappy and unwell. She had a whole host of health issues that were manifesting as serious acne all over her body. Renowned medical intuitive Louise Hay believes that acne is related to feelings of not accepting or liking yourself. I gave Megan some homework: to look in her eyes in the mirror and repeat the affirmation, "I love and accept myself wholeheartedly and unconditionally exactly as I am right now." She did it multiple times a day, and although at the start it brought her to tears she kept at it and the most magical thing started to happen . . . Her skin began to clear up. She was very skeptical at first, as she had tried everything. But, boy, was she glad she gave this a shot. Since then she has completely healed her acne and is now herself coaching young women with acne and self-confidence issues.

So be sure to utilize the potency of affirmations in your own life. Put them all around your house. Write them on Post-it Notes and stick them on your fridge or bathroom mirror; use them as your lock screen on your phone or your desktop background on your computer. You can set them as alarms on your phone and get them to go off several times throughout the day. You can also head to my website and download my free Soul Shares and stick them around your home or office.

2. *Quit picking on you!*

We are all going to stuff up, fall down, and make "mistakes" ... That's life! Striving for perfection is neither realistic nor healthy. What is "perfect" anyway? Your idea of perfect is different from someone else's, so let go of striving for perfection. Perfectionism is based on fear. Which means it's a perfect trigger for Mean Girl activity. When "bad" stuff happens, pick yourself up, dust yourself off, and cut yourself some slack, sister. Remember, there are no mistakes, just opportunities for evolution. Choose to see every "mistake" or "failure" as an opportunity for growth.

3. *Have your daily hour of love.*

Every day, do one thing for you. Whether it's going for a beautiful walk in nature, sitting and having a cup of herbal tea, calling your bestie for a chat, taking a bath, reading a book in the sunshine, or doing your favorite yoga class, schedule some time every day just for you. I like to call this the hour of love. I aim to have an hour in the afternoon; however, it doesn't always turn out that way and that's okay. Sometimes I only get fifteen minutes, but, hey, that's better than nothing, right? My hour of love is usually spent in the park barefoot just watching the world go by, and . . . wait for it . . . I am usually phone free. Holy smokes, Batman! You see, I—like lots of people—spend a lot of time in front of a computer and with my phone.

I am very sensitive to the radiation and EMFs they give off, so I need that time out to recharge with Mother Nature. This comes back to filling yourself up so that you are bursting with love. It's essential in order to live your best life.

4. *Get still.*

Did you know that we have between sixty and eighty thousand thoughts per day? That's a lot of Mean Girl chatter! We've discussed the importance of meditation, but if you're struggling with a formal practice, even just sitting in stillness for at least ten minutes each day will do you a world of good. Whether it's outside on a park bench, on the bus during your commute to work, or in the car before the school pickup, those precious minutes of solitude will change how your day unfolds.

So often those gaps of white spaces we have throughout our day are filled with social media stalking and constant e-mail checking (guilty!). Instead, next time you have a moment of white space, just sit, close your eyes, and breathe. You don't need to fill every moment: this creates no opening for miracles to occur.

5. *Pull yourself up.*

When you notice yourself buying into those old stories and limiting beliefs, catch yourself. Within that moment of awareness you have a choice to:

- Engage in those Mean Girl stories, or
- Flip 'em around.

For example, let's say the thought "I am not smart enough to start my own business" pops into your head. Reprogram that to "I am a smart and intelligent woman who is perfectly capable of following my heart and starting my dream business." Remember, the thoughts you choose to think are yours, and you have the freedom to choose again.

6. *Watch your Mean Girl.*

Your Mean Girl is super clever. She will sneak into your mind in her camouflage getup and plant seeds of self-doubt whenever she can. As soon as you spot the warning signs of her presence, or you catch her in the act, gently close the door on her, thank her for piping up, and remind her you are going to choose love instead.

7. *Let go.*

Letting go of hurt, pain, and anger is the key to your freedom. Letting go helps piece the hurt and shattered parts of your heart back together. Holding on to the past energetically attaches you to those old Mean Girl stories. Choose to let go and liberate yourself. When you let go of past hurt from someone else you are freeing yourself. You aren't necessarily condoning what the person did: you are simply freeing yourself from the ties that bind the two of you. (More on this later.)

8. *Stop playing small.*

There is only one you. And you, my darling, are *amazing*! Shine your bright light and show the world what you're made of. Your role on this planet is to share your unique gifts with the world and now is the time to do it.

Don't let your Mean Girl make you shrink; you are perfect just the way you are. You don't have to hide yourself to protect others' feelings. By you shining you actually allow them to shine also. Be brave and celebrate your greatness. In doing so, you liberate others to do the same.

Flex Your Self-Love Muscle Recap

- Self-love is not selfish: it is the very act of loving yourself wholeheartedly and unconditionally.
- Self-love is about cultivating a meaningful relationship with yourself.
- Flexing your self-love muscle is a daily practice, and through meditation and gratitude you are strengthening that muscle.
- Drop your expectations and open yourself up to spontaneity and magic.
- Gratitude creates more things to be grateful for.

Inspo-action

Flexing your self-love muscle is all about consistency. Fill out the Self-Love Menu to really hold yourself accountable.

Close your eyes, take in a few deep breaths, and start

to think about all the things that you love to do. Things that light you up from the inside out. Things that inspire the heck out of you, motivate you, and make you wanna yell, HELL. YEAH. BABY!

Once you have ten things, write them down:

_____

_____

_____

_____

_____

_____

_____

_____

_____

_____

Now that you have your ten things, it's your job to do at least one thing from this list every single day. (Bonus points if you do more.)

In moments when you want to down a tub of ice cream, a block of chocolate, or a bottle of wine, I want you to do something off your Self-Love Menu instead. The aim is that instead of filling yourself up from the outside in (which is what ice cream does), you start filling yourself up from the inside out (which is what the Self-Love Menu does).

Here's my Self-Love Menu:

- Watching the sunrise or sunset.
- Meditating in nature, either at the beach or in the park.
- Diving in the ocean.
- Hysterically belly laughing with my boys.
- Cooking a healthy organic meal and sharing it with all my loved ones.
- Reading a good book curled up in bed or soaking up the sun.
- Sipping organic herbal tea and having soulful conversations with my besties.
- Getting a mani-pedi or even a blow-dry (how good that feels!).
- Moving my body, either walking or doing yoga.
- Doing random acts of kindness.

Head to my website to get your free Self-Love Menu. Why don't you print it out, take a photo of it, and tag me on social media using the hashtag #masteringyour meangirl? I would *love* to see it.

THREE

dial up your worthy-o-meter

If you think dealing with issues like worthiness and
authenticity and vulnerability [is] not worthwhile
because there are more pressing issues, like the bottom
line or attendance or standardized test scores, you are
sadly, sadly mistaken. It underpins everything.

BRENÉ BROWN

Let's talk self-worth. Before I hit rock bottom and got my wake-up call, my worthy-o-meter was at an all-time low. I was trashing my body, ignoring my heart, and choosing fear, and I had no idea about the importance of owning my own worth. However, after years of choosing love over fear, flexing my self-love muscle, and mastering my Mean Girl, I have been able to really crank up my worthy-o-meter. Don't get me wrong, there are still moments when I forget—I am human and my Mean Girl still sometimes tells me I am not worthy of this wonderful relationship or the divine team I have around me—but I have gotten better at catching her in the act. I have sped up my comeback rate and I don't dwell on it like I used to. I simply see it for what it is, let it go, and remind myself of the truth, that I am worthy.

Your self-worth has such a major impact on how your life unfolds and what you attract into it. We are creating our lives moment by moment. Everyone's circumstances are different, but regardless, we can all choose to create a better tomorrow, whatever that may look like for you. For some that might mean creating your dream business and for others it might be as difficult as leaving an abusive relationship. But I don't believe anyone is more special than anyone else. I don't believe God, Buddha, Elvis (whoever you believe in) gave out any more specialness fairy dust to anyone when we came into this world. I believe it all comes down to worthiness! In fact, just the other day, my friend Nicole was telling me about her new job, which she loves, and she said to me, "I am so lucky to have this amazing job." I stopped her, looked her in the eyes, and said, "No! You're not lucky; you're so worthy of that job. Own your worth, sister!" After the initial shock of my statement wore off, she took a breath and said, "You're right, I am worthy of this. I deserve this job!" As soon as she said that her shoulders dropped an inch, she sat up taller, her eyes lit up, and her face became softer. I could see she really felt it in her heart.

It doesn't matter how much you want something—a soul mate, a new job, the money, the sports car, the beach house, the loyal tribe, the epic team—if you don't really, and I mean really, feel you are deeply worthy of those things, you will never attract them into your life. And if you do happen to call one of those things into your life it won't be sustainable: you will create it only to have it disappear in the blink of an eye because you didn't really feel like you were one hundred percent worthy of it to begin with. Worthiness matters and is the first quality you need to acknowledge in yourself in order to call in what you truly desire in life.

One of my clients, Gemma, had just landed her dream job at a well-regarded advertising agency. She poured her heart and soul into her presentation and worked really hard to land the job. However, there were a few things she said in our coaching sessions that were warning signs to me that she didn't really feel she was one hundred percent worthy of this job. I mentioned this to her and she agreed she didn't completely feel she was deserving of it. She started doing my worthiness meditation every day and I got her to work on dialing up her worthy-o-meter, but it was too late to shift her energy with that particular job. Within a few months, she was fired. She was devastated and told me she could never get her worthy-o-meter to a ten because at her core, she didn't believe she was good enough to experience the kind of professional success she craved. It was a big thing to admit (and like I always say, awareness is the first step in creating change). So from that point on, we began working on ingraining a feeling of sincere worthiness at a deep-down cellular level—so she really feels it in her heart and gut—and she has since landed another dream job that she truly loves and has been able to keep.

Living your dream life bursting with love has everything to do with worthiness.

I know some of the most financially "lucky" and "blessed" people who suffer depression and are very unhappy. I also know people without much financial wealth at all who live lives of incredible abundance.

You get what you feel you deserve, and if that's a million dollars or your soul mate, then, great, enjoy it and really own it. But if it's something else, take a look at how well you're doing on your worthy-o-meter. You might need to do some work to dial it back up to a ten. And remember, your Mean Girl is going to pop up and tell you you aren't worthy of that great job, amazing guy, loyal tribe, pay raise, or peak health. Your Mean Girl wants to keep you hanging out in Fear Town. But you don't belong there! You belong in a mansion in Love City: that's your truth—but only if you truly believe it to be.

Your life experiences have everything to do with where you sit on the worthy-o-meter.

When I first got together with my hubby, I remember catching myself saying, "I am so lucky. I feel so blessed." He stopped me immediately and said, "No you're not, honey, you're so worthy. You deserve all this happiness and love you're experiencing right now, but you gotta believe it." My Mean Girl's immediate reaction was to tell me, "No, you don't." Straight to the jugular. But thankfully I knew enough about her tricky little games to stop her in her tracks. I do deserve happiness and love! I truly do. And so do you, beautiful.

The truth is, everything happens for a reason. Tough pill to swallow, I know, but there are nuggets of wisdom in everything: we just have to dig for them.

This feeling of worthiness is reflected in all three major areas of your life—your health, wealth, and love. Someone who owns their worth and has their worthy-o-meter at ten will be experiencing life very differently from someone who's hovering around zero. It's all relative to where you sit on the meter.

So, how worthy do you feel right now? If you desire good health, do you really feel you are worthy of it? If you desire love, do you really feel you are worthy of deep affection? If you desire abundance, is your worthy-o-meter really cranked up to ten? If the answer is no, or anything less than a ten, then you don't need to fix, change, or improve anything outside of yourself, my darling. All you have to do is work on dialing up your internal worthy-o-meter. Really own your worth. Feel it in your bones. Let go of any limiting Mean Girl beliefs and allow yourself to experience what it really feels like to be truly worthy from your very core. Feel it with every cell in your entire body—you cannot manifest your heart's desires until your worthy-o-meter is maxed out. Even being at a nine is not enough: your worthiness needs to be at a ten or, even better, off the Richter scale. The best part is you can get there right now—all you have to do is really own it.

Inspo-action

Let's dial up your worthy-o-meter right now. Take a moment to write down twenty things that you are *excellent* at. Twenty might seem like a lot, I know, but trust me— you can do it! It can be things that are big or small, things that seem important or even silly . . . The point of the exercise is to dwell on and linger in all your positive qualities, rather than focusing on the negative ones, as so many of us normally do.

I'll go first.

I'm excellent at . . .

- Reading books to Leo (he loves when I put on silly voices!).

- Writing (it took me a while to own this one, but now I stand in it, loud and proud!).

- Cooking, especially delicious healthy dishes and raw desserts (yum!).

- Dancing.

- Organizing projects and team members (it helps that I have a fab team around me!).

- Doing silly stuff to make people laugh (I'm always up for a lounge-room karaoke session or an office dance-off).

- Ringing my mum and dad just to chat.

- Practicing self-care.

- Saying no and setting boundaries (this one didn't come naturally to me at first, but I'm proud of it now!).

- Setting a beautiful table and creating a gorgeous welcoming atmosphere for our guests.

- Public speaking.

- Articulating my vision.

- Manifesting.

- Breaking big-picture things down into manageable chunks.

- Being present with my beautiful husband (although I work on it daily).

- Giving little gifts to the people I love, just because.

- De-cluttering and organizing.

- Getting things finished and ticked off my to-do list.

- Creating products, programs, and events that serve and inspire my beautiful tribe.

- Holding space for people—clients, loved ones, soul sisters, tribe members, and my team.

Now it's your turn.

I'm excellent at . . .

_____   _____

_____   _____

_____   _____

_____   _____

_____   _____

_____   _____

_____   _____

_____   _____

_____   _____

_____   _____

_____   _____

_____   _____

_____   _____

_____   _____

_____   _____

_____   _____

_____   _____

_____   _____

_____   _____

To really amp up your self-worth, read this list to yourself every day, and try to add something new to it each week. Concentrate on that awesome feeling that rises within you whenever you think about all these things you're amazing at. Invite more of that wonderful feeling into your life.

You can also head over to my website to check out the special worthiness meditation I've created just for you. Do this worthiness meditation daily for maximum effect and watch what happens in your life when you dial up your self-worth. You'll find that everything starts to flow a whole lot more effortlessly. Good things will suddenly start appearing out of nowhere, without explanation. Don't try to fight it or analyze it; just flow with it.

Take Out the Trash

Everything you can imagine is real.

PABLO PICASSO

Back when I was in the clutches of my Mean Girl, I couldn't believe that I was responsible for what I was creating in my life. It was a very bitter pill for me to swallow. I didn't have anything to do with my ex-boyfriend cheating on me; it wasn't my fault that I got sick; I couldn't help it if I had no money. Nothing was ever my responsibility: I was just the victim.

It took me a while to fully grasp the concept that my limiting Mean Girl beliefs had created all those circumstances in my life. It's confronting! But the truth is, I had unconsciously invited hardship and turmoil into my life so that I could learn the lessons I needed to learn. Although I may not have been the one actually doing the cheating, I was the one who'd allowed herself to become deeply involved with someone who did not have her best interests at heart. I was the one who hadn't listened to her gut in the first place. And I was the one who hadn't stood up for herself. It all boiled down to me. Yes, I loved my boyfriend (or so I thought), but when I started going out with him, my intuition told me he was a bit of a player—a wild boy—and maybe not the best choice for me. But he was so good-looking and charming and cute and funny, I was flattered by his attention, and I stifled all my doubts and concerns.

Similarly, I kind of knew that eating and drinking processed crap wasn't good for me—but, hey, I was "busy," right? With this "amazing" career and life that had me burning the candle at both ends, I didn't have time to look after myself and I didn't really care. That's what I mean about creating the circumstances in my life. No one forced me to go out with the player or fuel my body with junk or take those unfulfilling jobs. It was all me and my limiting beliefs: they were my decisions. I just heard all my Mean Girl excuses and didn't listen to my heart. I needed to put on my big-girl pants, take some responsibility for how my life was unfolding, and send my old limiting beliefs to the trash.

Some people might run away from that realization. But once I'd got my head around it, I embraced it. It's exciting when you finally realize that you are the director, producer, and leading actor of your own life movie. Seriously, how cool is that? And because we're all playing our own starring roles, we get to create our own lives exactly how we want them, moment by moment. You have the power, my darling. Even more than that, your actions today affect your life tomorrow. This can be confronting for some people because it means they have to take responsibility for their future. For others, it's incredibly liberating to realize that they are the one in the driver's seat. However you feel, it's the truth: you are the one responsible for how your life pans out. No one else . . . just you!

This also means that the phrase "It isn't fair" (or "Life's not fair") is now eliminated from your vocabulary. These attitudes are so self-defeating and useless. All you are doing is expanding negative energy that is not serving you or anyone around you. But now you know how to put your big-girl pants on and are empowered to take full responsibility for yourself and your life. How awesome!

Every moment is a clean slate, a fresh start, a new opportunity to be your best. Give it your all, show up fully, and choose love.

How do you feel right now? Are you excited by the fact that you are creating your life moment by moment? Or did you just gulp at the thought that you now have to take responsibility?

Whatever it is you're feeling, know that it is perfect and you are exactly where you need to be right now. But let's take some action to step things up . . .

Inspo-action

Take a moment now to answer these two questions:

What are you creating in your life right now that isn't supporting you?

_____

_____

_____

What limiting Mean Girl beliefs can you take to the trash can? What sentences are swirling around and around in your head, keeping you bogged in powerlessness? I am not smart enough to land the job; I will never lose the tummy fat; I can't follow my passion or start my dream business; I will never find my soul mate; I will never get out of debt; I will never feel well and vital again; I will never find my soul sisters . . . Whatever they are for you, write them down. It's time to take these limiting beliefs to the trash.

_____

_____

_____

A big part of stepping into your power and relinquishing your limiting beliefs is quitting the victim role—for good! We have a "no pity party" rule in our house. If you are playing the victim, you get sent straight to the balcony—that energy is not welcome. It's usually me that gets sent there the most. The first time Nick banished me to the balcony I was in a real huff, but as soon as I got out there I started laughing at how ridiculously I was behaving. You can't help but laugh when your partner is sending you to the "pity party sin bin"! In that moment, I realized I was playing the victim and decided to return to love and the present moment.

Maybe you can incorporate a pity party sin bin into your home too. Your Mean Girl won't like it, but it's a great tool to stop her in her tracks.

Stop Playing Small

There is no passion to be found playing small—in settling for a life that is less than the one you are capable of living.
NELSON MANDELA

Don't let your limiting Mean Girl thoughts tell you that you're not worthy of the love, health, and abundance you desire. That's a load of BS. You are absolutely worthy of all the love, health, and happiness in the world. We all are! All you have to do is believe it. And I mean really believe it, with every bone in your body and every fiber of your being. Let it radiate out of every single pore and pulse through your veins. Have fun with it and dream big. You decide the course of your life. You decide which direction it takes. You decide the beginning, middle, and ending. You decide whether you are creating a master-piece or a messterpiece, my love. How exciting is that?!

Inspo-action

In your life right now, are you dreaming big or playing small? Why not dream big? If your Mean Girl is loudly telling you you're not worthy of big things, it's time to put that to bed and really turn your desires into reality. It's time to dial up your worthy-o-meter and live the life of your dreams. Write down exactly how you want your health, wealth, and love to be right now. Remember, nothing is off-limits!

_____

_____

_____

_____

_____

_____

_____

_____

Self-Sabotage and Your Mean Girl

When you first set your internal GPS to _love_, you're going to encounter some pretty heavy artillery fire from your Mean Girl. This is when she usually rears her head hard and fast. Your job is not to let her win. She doesn't want you to shine, to be happy, or to be present. Why? Because that's your Mean Girl's job—to keep you stuck in Fear

Town. If you're not in Fear Town she can't plant seeds of doubt in your mind. And let me tell you, she's going to try really hard to take you down.

I've seen it happen many times. One of my clients, Bella, had finally met this amazing guy she was really into. They had been on several dates and things were getting pretty serious, but before he could ask her to go "official," her Mean Girl popped up and said, "This guy is too good to be true; it won't work." Before she knew it, she'd canceled the next date. Soon after, she realized that she was self-sabotaging and that she had just let go of an amazing guy. She tried to call him back but it was already too late—he was no longer interested. Was this a missed opportunity for Bella? She will never know because in that moment she chose to listen to her Mean Girl, and as a result the potential relationship never got to fully express itself.

Another client, Donna, was going for a big job interview. She knew she'd nailed the interview, but, on the way out, her Mean Girl stepped in and she said something really silly to the CEO of the company. The comment cost her the job. Later, when she was reflecting over what had happened, she realized she was in flow and being her authentic self during the entire interview except for that second right at the very end when she started doubting herself. That was when she exited the present moment and her Mean Girl joined the party and the comment slipped out. In that moment, she left her heart and the present moment. That is the Mean Girl's primary role—to remove you from the here and now and get you caught up in your head, either going back to the past or worrying over the future.

My Mean Girl often tries to sabotage my relationship. I have the most divine husband and our relationship is beyond my wildest dreams, but sometimes—usually when everything is going great—she will drop in some old programming and start saying, "This is too good to be true; something bad is going to happen." My Mean Girl will start to look for problems or issues—for example, getting angry with him over not hanging up the bath mat or leaving his clothes on the floor. Ridiculous, I know, but this is what your Mean Girl is capable of. We have to be sharp and on our A game to catch her wily ways and sneaky tricks. It's our job to be highly alert and stop her when she drops the self-sabotage bomb on us.

Exiting the present moment is a form of self-sabotage. When you close the door to the present, you open the door to your past.

I used to self-sabotage with food. I would actually use it as a form of self-harm. I would be "good" and "eat well" all week and then, when something happened outside of my control, I would binge as a way of harming myself. It was a vicious cycle of self-sabotage and not a pleasant way to live.

I now see and use food as nourishment. Everything I put into my body is of the highest quality and purest form. I now respect my temple and want to nurture and look after it. After all, we only get one.

I also see a lot of self-sabotage with women and their bodies, the ongoing tortuous internal monologue of "I hate my thighs," "My stomach is repulsive," and "My upper arms are so wobbly." This then carries over into conversations outside your head. A friend tells you that you look beautiful, to which you reply, "Oh no, my hair needs doing and I've put on weight." Why do we do that? Someone pays us a compliment and instead of taking it in and saying thank you, our immediate reaction is to self-sabotage. This has got to stop! This type of behavior is not just boring: it's actively feeding your Mean Girl. Not only that, your children are watching and will mimic your neuroses. So if you want your children to think poorly about themselves, by all means—keep going. But if you want better for them, let's start to reprogram that, quick smart.

Inspo-action

Where in your life right now are you self-sabotaging? Is it in your relationship with your partner, your work, your finances, how you move your body, or the food you eat?

Where are you robbing yourself and selling yourself short?

_____

_____

_____

Remember, you deserve the absolute best, my darling. Don't let your Mean Girl or anyone else tell you otherwise. Be mindful of the areas you self-sabotage and let's quit that right now. In order to live your wildest dreams and master your Mean Girl, you need to put that to bed and start acting in your own highest interest.

Opposites Attract

What you resist persists. What you look at disappears.

NEALE DONALD WALSCH, *Conversations with God*

There is a common misconception that if we want something badly enough, it will magically turn up in our laps on a silver platter. The law of attraction, right?

I remember wanting so desperately to get the leading lady roles, but my hunger for it—and my fear that I might not get the job—just made it harder to land the roles. The casting directors could smell my desperation from a mile away (definitely not the most desirable trait!) and it always ended up costing me the part. The times when I did go into a casting feeling open and unattached to the outcome were the occasions I landed the roles. It ain't rocket science.

You see, desperately wanting something comes from fear—fear of the opposite of what you actually think you "want." For example, you want good health because you're scared to get sick or maybe even scared of death. You want financial abundance because you're scared you won't be able to provide for your family. You want a soul mate because you want someone to fill an emotional void within you.

It is this desperate wanting of something that repels it away from you.

The key is to remain neutral. You have to be okay with both outcomes and have the courage to accept what you don't want as well. Accept the fear of the opposite of what you think you want.

It all comes down to preferences and desires. I have a preference that it's sunny tomorrow, but if it's not I am still okay with that outcome. I have a desire that my flight be on time, but if it's not I am still okay with that outcome. I have a preference that Leo will not wake up during the night, but I am still okay if he does. I am not going to lose it and become a crazy woman if I don't get my preference; I will remain neutral either way. Every situation is neutral until you attach a label to it. I believe that you have to take inspired action toward what you desire and be okay with both outcomes. You have to want something with all your heart and soul—not your head—but accept the opposite also.

It has now been scientifically proven by many scientists around the world that all matter in the Universe is energy, and fear vibrates at a different frequency than love. So when I walked into my auditions vibrating with fear, of course that was what I was going to manifest. Ditto for dates, job interviews, and everything else. Instead of approaching all these situations out of fear, approach them from a place of love. Simply focus on the fact that you would love to experience vibrant health, financial freedom, abundance, or a connection with your soul mate . . . and not because you are scared of what you don't want.

When you are hanging out with your Mean Girl you attract what you fear, and you repel what you truly desire.

A few years ago, I was about to head away on a family holiday to Bali. The week before our trip, I started to feel a little niggle in my throat, which had me running scared—I so desperately didn't want to get sick. I kept telling myself to keep pushing through the tired ness and the little niggles, and I was loading up on vitamin C and probiotic foods in order to kill off any nasty bugs that were lurking around. But I wasn't doing it out of a desire to honor my temple: I was doing it out of fear of getting sick. Of course, you can probably guess how things unfolded. Once we got to our hotel, it all caught up with me, and I was in bed with a fever (and the rest of it) for the whole trip. I was so scared of it happening that of course it was going to play out. The week before I left, when I first felt that little inkling of being run-down, if I had just opened my heart, completely surrendered, and looked at what was going on, most likely my body would have just done its natural thing to detox whatever was going on inside me. But because I deliberately tried to fight it and resist it with fear, it persisted with full force and completely floored me.

It's important to note that there's nothing to fear about getting sick or feeling unwell. It's just your body detoxifying, letting go, and giving you a message. Don't shoot the messenger; instead, listen to it.

You have to remember that the very act of so desperately wanting something is going to push it away. Back in my early twenties when I had my heart broken, I remember so desperately wanting him to take me back. I tried everything; I even begged him, but he still turned me down. (No wonder, really—who wants to be with someone who's that desperate?) Looking back, I have to laugh, because there is no way in the world I would act like that today (which goes to show how far I've come). Desperately wanting something or someone is a very unattractive quality that comes from fear and is only going to push away the very thing you think you want.

Inspo-action

What do you so desperately want in your life right now? Are you wanting it out of fear or pure desire?

_____

_____

_____

_____

_____

Let go of the fear-based wants and the stomach-squirming desperation, and simply allow your heart to desire from a place of love. There's a big difference.

Worthy-O-Meter Recap

- How worthy you feel is reflected in all areas of your life.
- You are the director, producer, and leading lady of your own life movie. Get creative and play big.
- Your actions today affect your life tomorrow.
- You create your life moment by moment. If you don't like what you're creating, you can create again.
- Don't let your Mean Girl self-sabotage. You deserve all the love, health, and happiness in the world.
- What you resist persists; what you look at and face head-on disappears.

Letter to Your Future Self

Write a letter to your future self, one year from today. Answer these questions in depth: What are you doing? Where are you living? How is your health? Who is surrounding you? What are you doing for work? How do you feel? How are you contributing your gifts to the world?

Once you've finished your letter, print it off and stick it on your fridge or on your vision board so you can constantly be inspired and motivated for your mission.

Make Love Your Internal GPS Checklist

Now that you've finished part one of this book, you know how to set your internal GPS squarely on the love end of the spectrum. The following affirmations represent what you've learned so far and will remind you to integrate this wisdom into your daily life. Head to my website and print them out, stick them somewhere you'll see them frequently, and check in with them every day.

☐ I choose love over fear in every moment.

☐ I flex my self-love muscle every day.

☐ I take action daily to dial up my worthy-o-meter.

PART TWO

Living from Love

FOUR

being fabulously healthy

You can set yourself up to be sick, or you
can choose to stay well.

WAYNE DYER

How we feed and treat our bodies is a direct reflection of how we feel about ourselves.

Someone who's passionate about her work, is surrounded by people she loves, and is at a solid ten on the worthy-o-meter is going to treat her body very differently compared to someone who hates her job, feels like the world is against her, is surrounded by unhealthy relationships, and is constantly entertaining her Mean Girl.

How you feel about yourself is reflected in every choice you make and every action you take.

When I think back to my early twenties, my food choices said a lot about my internal state. I wanted quick, easy, and cheap options. Not only did I not understand the importance of nourishing my body, I didn't believe I was worth anything more than that. Now, however, I choose foods that are local, organic, fresh, wholesome, and nourishing. Everything that enters my mouth is of the highest quality and purest form. Why? Because I understand that it is my sacred duty to nourish the temple I have been given. Looking after myself in this way has actually become one of my greatest pleasures in life.

The body is the temple of your spirit and processed and packaged "foods" made in factories for profit will not nourish you, but food from nature will. Food from Mother Earth is a gift from love.

Inspo-action

Take a moment now and reflect on how you nourish your body. Are you picking the cheapest and quickest options, or are you giving yourself the most loving, high-quality, high-vibrational foods you can find?

Honor yourself enough to take the time to prepare something nourishing with love. Sit down without distractions, give thanks to your food, and enjoy it. Food is there to be enjoyed and to be fun. Don't take it too seriously, and have fun creating in the kitchen—either alone or with your family—and don't let your Mean Girl tell you you aren't worthy of fresh, wholesome foods, because you absolutely are.

From Enemies to Besties with Food

Before we even get into which foods are actually good for you, I believe it's way more important to look at your relationship with food itself. I've said it before and I'll say it again: everything outside us is a reflection of our internal state. Nowhere is this truer than in our health and well-being. If you're waging an internal war with your Mean Girl against every morsel you eat, you're setting yourself up for some pretty serious health issues—a fact I know all too well!

As I've said, before I hit rock bottom, I had quite a destructive relationship with food. Basically, I hated it. I loathed every aspect of it and didn't really want anything to do with it.

Can you relate?

I saw food as the enemy. I would binge on sugar, alcohol, and refined carbohydrates but deprive myself of any real nutrition. For breakfast I would go to a coffee chain and get a large caramel latte with extra cream, caramel sauce, and chocolate on top. Lunch would consist of a bag of yogurt- or chocolate-covered dried fruit and nuts I would pick up at the tube station. Then dinner would be grilled processed tofu with low-fat bottled sweet chili sauce (please do not try this at home!). Basically, I didn't care about myself and would take drastic measures to try to look like the Victoria's Secret models. I was also constantly experimenting with the latest fad diet and weight-loss pills . . . anything to be thin, keep the weight off, and feel accepted. I was also quite stingy and didn't want to "waste" my money on food, so I always opted for the cheap route . . . Not exactly ideal when it comes to your health!

This went on for years, until my body could no longer cope and decided to close up shop. At the time, I didn't realize it was because of the way I was treating myself, but looking back it's a complete reflection of my internal state. I didn't value the importance of food and the effect it had on my physical and emotional health, and I paid the consequences.

SO WHY WAS FOOD THE ENEMY?

Food was the enemy because I was desperately unhappy and needed something to blame and to control. It was much easier to blame something external than take responsibility and look within. Can you imagine? I was miserable, sick, depressed, anxious, and suffering from panic attacks—there was no way in hell I wanted to be responsible for all of that! Of course, the truth was that I was the one manifesting everything. But for years I wasn't ready to face that reality and bear the responsibility.

As I lay in the hospital, with a faceful of cold sores, dosed up on morphine, I finally had no choice but to take a long, hard look at what was going on. I was sick and tired of depriving my body and feeling the way I did. My body was lacking vital nutrients and I was so over feeling constantly exhausted. It was time to take responsibility and reclaim my power.

When I got honest with myself, I realized that whenever I was unhappy or something felt out of my control, I would turn to sugar, refined carbs, processed foods, and other "foodlike substances"— definitely not made with love—in order to fill that uncomfortable void deep within.

And I was unhappy and unwell a lot.

This realization triggered some big internal changes. In fact, my eating habits swung a full hundred and eighty degrees. But unlike the crash diets I'd been on in the past, these changes came about slowly and organically. You see, instead of obsessing about each mouthful that entered my body, I decided to start addressing the emotional stuff first. As I slowly but surely started to be aware of my Mean Girl and her crazy little games, I started to make some internal shifts, and my eating habits naturally began to recalibrate and realign. I started to lean toward high-vibrational wholesome food made with love and care. My body began craving organic, fresh, home-cooked meals. And I found pleasure in eating for nourishment and wellness, something I'd never experienced before.

After eating this way for years now, I've experienced so many other benefits too. Not only did changing my diet allow me to heal from acne, eczema, depression, anxiety, and severe cold sore outbreaks, I also have more stable energy levels than I've ever had before. Without the massive sugar-induced highs and lows, my moods no longer fluctuate and bottom out. And I've settled into my ideal weight for my body and am able to maintain it with ease—no drastic yo-yo dieting, deprivation, or limiting myself. I actually haven't dieted since. The way I eat now is my way of life.

I now look at food with such love and appreciation. I use it to nourish my temple. I tune in and eat what my body asks for in order to function at optimal levels. And I'm so grateful to have access to delicious, high-quality food—organic fruits and vegetables, grass-fed (and grass-finished) ethically raised animal products, and wild-caught fish. I now love and respect my body so much that I take the time to understand where my food has come from. I go to the farms and chat to my fishmonger and butcher to find out as much as possible about their products so I can make the most informed decision for myself and my family.

Inspo-action

Because what you eat is such a direct reflection of your internal state, looking at your eating habits can tell you a lot about yourself.

It's time to get honest. Take a moment to think about your relationship with food and write down your answers to the following questions:

Are you enemies or besties with food?

_____

Did you reach for junk food, sugar, or caffeine when you felt tired or stressed out this past week?

_____

Are you turning to processed, fast, or ready-to-eat foods because you're "too busy" to prepare nourishing meals?

_____

Do you often skip meals or "forget to eat"?

_____

Do you tend to snack all through the day or always crave something sweet after a meal?

_____

When you ate dinner last night, were you watching TV, scrolling Facebook, or stalking someone on Instagram?

_____

Now that we know where you're at, it's time to delve deeper and start looking at the underlying beliefs that influence the way we eat.

How to Heal Your Relationship with Food

The best way to heal your relationship with food is to start by bringing awareness to your eating habits. There's one simple question that can help you turn everything around: "Am I eating out of love or fear?"

If the answer is love, then keep going. Enjoy your food, give thanks for it, and be present while you enjoy your nourishing meal.

If the answer is fear, stop and ask yourself, "What's really going on here?" Notice the emotions and Mean Girl talk that is going on inside your head. What is your Mean Girl saying to you? Is she judging you? Are you feeling guilty or angry with yourself? Does your Mean Girl want to punish you for overeating last night after dinner, or for not going to the gym this morning?

Now I want you to take a deep belly breath and let all that go. Let's take one more, and on the exhale let it all out and accept exactly what is, right now.

No matter how screwed up your eating habits may feel right now, it doesn't mean you have to entertain a torturous relationship with food forever. That's boring! All we need to do is a little mental reprogramming around food. Let's deliberately and consciously choose to reframe your thoughts with this affirmation:

"I easily and willingly choose nourishing, fresh, healthy foods that are grown and prepared with love. I choose to nurture and nourish my beautiful temple."

If it helps, you could write this on a Post-it Note and stick it on your bathroom mirror or your fridge or set it as a phone reminder for when those three p.m. cravings creep up. And next time you go to make less-desirable food choices, try my powerful step-by-step guide to healing your relationship with food and making peace with your meals.

STEP 1: Tune in with yourself. Next time you go to reach for a tub of ice cream or a block of chocolate, ask yourself, "What's really going on here? What emotions am I trying to suppress with food right now?"

STEP 2: Notice what emotions and/or feelings arise for you and sit with them. Remember, you are not your emotions or feelings. They are just energy moving around your body and they need to be released. So don't let your Mean Girl try to jump in and attach stories to them. Stay very present and breathe.

STEP 3: Allow the emotions to just be there and to unfold however they are supposed to. Try not to interfere and don't let your Mean Girl judge them; just allow them to be and feel them fully and completely.

STEP 4: If you feel called to journal about how you're feeling, please do so now. But whatever you do, don't run away with the story. You must stay very present in order to transcend these unresolved feelings; otherwise, they'll just keep coming back time and time again. And you're too busy living your wildest dreams for that.

Choose this practice every time you feel the urge to suppress your emotions with a bag of sweets or a packet of biscuits. Keep working on it and soon it will become habit. Eventually it will become a natural way of life, but like anything it takes practice so be patient and persistent. You're worth the effort, though! You and your body deserve to be loved, nourished, and nurtured. Let's heal your relationship with food, once and for all.

Nourish Your Temple

The body never lies.

MARTHA GRAHAM

Now that we've discussed your relationship with food, it's time to take a closer look at the food itself and exactly what is going to help you thrive.

There is so much information about food out there, it's enough to do your head in. There's a gazillion diets proclaiming to work miracles, there's loads of confusing and conflicting information about what we should or shouldn't be eating, and the supermarket shelves are packed with fancy products and supplements that all overpromise and underdeliver. No wonder people get overwhelmed and confused!

Unlike most books about health and well-being, I'm not going to tell you what you should and shouldn't eat. I firmly believe that nobody knows what you should be eating better than you—all of us have unique lifestyles and nutritional requirements, and there's no one way of eating that suits everyone. I will, however, share with you how I have healed myself and what has worked for my clients and family. These principles are tried and true, but I strongly encourage you to play around with them and figure out what's right for you. Tap into your intuition and listen to your body, as it always knows best.

My Food Philosophy

CAUTION: THE INFORMATION YOU ARE ABOUT TO READ IS NOT WHAT WE ARE TAUGHT IN SCHOOL!

- Eat local, organic, fresh, whole, in-season produce, preferably from your farmers' market or grown yourself.
- Avoid refined sugar, wheat, dairy, gluten, soy, caffeine, alcohol, and processed and packaged foodlike substances as much as you possibly can.
- Add in loads of easy-to-digest cooked vegetables, some low-GI (glycemic index) fruits (like berries), and plenty of enzyme-rich light salad vegetables.
- Eat the rainbow. Try to get as many different-colored veggies on your plate as possible.
- Sip plenty of room-temperature filtered or spring water during the day. Carry around a stainless steel water bottle and refill it where you can. Unfiltered tap water is a big no-no unless you are hooked into a spring.
- If you are going to have nuts, seeds, and grains, make sure you soak and activate them before eating. However,

if you have gut issues or are healing your gut, it is recommended to keep these foods to a bare minimum. I know what you're thinking: What? No quinoa, pumpkin seed, and goji berry salads? That's right, beautiful—these foods are not a major part of my food philosophy. You can, however, try reintroducing them in small doses once your guts are running like a well-(coconut)-oiled machine. (See next point if you are vegan.)

- Follow the 80/20 rule—80 percent of your plate should be mostly cooked vegetables and 20 percent protein. If you are vegan, switch the 20 percent to grainlike seeds such as quinoa, millet, or amaranth.

- Aim to eat something green with every meal. Green veggies are your friends, as they are incredibly detoxifying and immune boosting.

- Ever wonder why some people seem to have such shiny hair and clear eyes? Fermented veggies, baby! Include some of these probiotic- and enzyme-rich foods with each meal to enhance digestion and clean up any leftover undigested waste material.

- Cook with vitamin Love. Yep, vitamin L is the most important ingredient you can add. Make sure you are infusing all your food with love. This might sound a little cray-cray, but I talk to my food and tell my food how grateful I am to have access to it. Give it a go!

- Try to eat organic or chemical free whenever possible. It really makes a difference because the organic produce hasn't been sprayed with chemicals and pesticides, and organic animal products haven't been pumped full of antibiotics and growth hormones. I believe you can't put a price on your health and well-being. And eating chemical free or organic will save you loads of moolah on doctors and medications down the track.

- All red meat should be grass fed, grass finished, and from a trusted source. Do your research and ask your butcher. If they don't know where their produce has come from or are vague in their answers, run for the hills, sister!

- All poultry and pork should be free range (or pastured) and fed their natural diet (not corn). Again, make sure you ask your butcher.

- All fish should be wild caught, not farmed. Ask your fishmonger, and if they don't know, go somewhere else or head out with your fishing rod and catch your own.

- Eat nose-to-tail, including the bone marrow, cartilage, organs, and skin (it's loaded with collagen, which is great for your skin). Muscle meat is more acidic, whereas organs and marrow are more alkaline, so eating nose-to-tail is a more pH-balanced approach. Eating nose-to-tail is also a lot cheaper than buying the expensive cuts of meat.

- Cook meat on the bone whenever possible. Not only will your meal be juicy and delicious, you'll also get the added minerals and nutrients from the bone, and you can then use the leftover bones to make bone broth (mm-mm). Which brings us to . . .

- Drink a cup of bone or vegetable broth daily to really supercharge your way toward shiny hair, sexy skin, and humming hormones.

- I also strongly believe in food combining. It makes total sense that some foods are not meant to be eaten together—for example, a steak isn't meant to be eaten with a bowl of fruit, and grains don't mix well with protein. The reason I got interested in food combining was because I kept noticing that after I ate certain things, I became really bloated and uncomfortable. When I started to implement food-combining principles into my life, the bloating and discomfort disappeared; I even lost weight and my overall health dramatically improved. For more information you can read *The Body Ecology Diet* by Donna Gates.

I understand buying organic produce isn't as cheap as conventional produce, but I have found ways to keep the cost down, and in some cases it works out about the same if not cheaper to eat organic, plus it's loads better for you.

Four ways to keep the cost down:

1. Head to the farmers' market when it is about to close, as most stalls will cut their prices by half.
2. Grow your own produce in your backyard or start with a few herbs on your windowsill.
3. If you grow your own, you can swap and trade with your neighbors who also grow produce. If you grow

tomatoes and they grow cucumbers, swap so you can mix it up.

4. Join a community garden where you get your own bed.

It might sound like a lot of work, but planting the seeds, watering them, and watching them grow, then taking your produce home to cook and enjoy with your loved ones, is incredibly rewarding and very educational for the kiddies.

Like everything in this book, try the suggestions that resonate most with you and see how they make you feel. If something doesn't feel great, then stop—at least you know more about your body. If it does feel good, brilliant—you just found another secret weapon to add to your wellness arsenal. It's also important you seek professional medical advice before you try any of these suggestions.

Whatever your nutritional preferences, please remember that it's your birthright to feel well, vital, healthy, and strong; don't let your Mean Girl use food to sabotage you. You were born to thrive, flourish, and feel fabulously healthy.

Inspo-action

Now it's time for you to take some inspired action.

Head into your kitchen, open your pantry and fridge, and take note of anything that is packaged and processed, and next time buy the whole food alternative or, if you want to go cold turkey, throw out everything that's in a packet or box that is full of preservatives, colors, flavors, and additives. Check the ingredients list on everything. It's time to get serious about nourishing your temple so you can feel fabulously healthy . . . for good!

The Truth about Cravings

When people are trying to create new eating habits, one of the most common roadblocks they encounter is food cravings, specifically sugar cravings. That hankering for something sweet at the end of a meal or as an afternoon pick-me-up can be so overwhelming, it can potentially derail all your good intentions. But if you understand why these cravings arise, you can be better equipped to ward them off.

After much research with myself and my clients I have found these to be the three most common reasons for sugar cravings:

1. *Habit*

    If you reach for a chocolate bar every day at three p.m., your body gets used to it. It's muscle memory. It becomes a habit and gets ingrained in your brain. Most of the time, if you really tune in and get super honest with yourself, you'll discover you don't actually really even feel like one at all, it's just a habit and your Mean Girl trying to sabotage you. If this sounds like you, make sure you're aware of your eating patterns and consciously tune in and listen to your body—that's the key to busting out of habit. And remember, breaking a habit takes commitment and practice—you can't just do it once and expect to be perfect. You have to work on it every time it pops up. Twenty-one days is often quoted as being the length of time it takes to properly break an old habit (or cement a new one) so give it a go for that long and see how you feel. I think you'll find yourself pleasantly surprised!

2. *Boredom*

How often have you craved sugar when—if you were totally honest with yourself—you were just bored? When we've got nothing to do, it's oh so easy to walk into the kitchen, open the pantry, and grab a box of biscuits . . . because why the heck not? In these instances, you're usually not even hungry and most likely just filling an emotional void. Sitting with your feelings is far more constructive than random fridge surfing or pantry prowling. Use the powerful four-step "heal your relationship with food" technique I previously mentioned to combat boredom eating.

3. *Dehydration*

Lots of cravings are the result of being dehydrated. Next time you feel a hankering for sugar, try having a massive glass of water first, then reassess your cravings. You'll be surprised how often they simply disappear. Reaching for sugary snacks is never a good option. It's your Mean Girl's way of looking for comfort and love, but, as with drugs or alcohol, the euphoria quickly melts away and the side effects are terrible.

As I have mentioned many times before, when it comes to food, it's super important to tune in to your body. Real cravings are your body speaking to you loud and clear, so make sure you listen up and use them as an opportunity to dive deeper within yourself and not suppress your emotions.

It's Not Just about What You Eat . . .

It's also about what you drink.

Back in my party-girl days, I drank a lot. I used alcohol to suppress my feelings and to give me confidence in social situations. I remember always having to have a drink (or three) at home first before I went out so that I would feel confident enough to walk into the bar. I was so unhappy in my life that I looked forward to getting blind drunk on Saturday nights to numb the pain. I wasn't an alcoholic, but I undeniably wasn't treating myself in a loving way, that's for sure. My worthy-o-meter was definitely at zero.

I remember many times being escorted from nightclubs kicking and screaming because I was "too intoxicated" . . . *Says who?* I thought at the time. Or the time I was so drunk I slipped on the dance floor while busting some serious moves to Beyoncé's "Single Ladies," sprained my ankle, and had to be carried out by a bouncer. (I should also mention that that particular night I was wearing a rather small miniskirt and I am sure it was around my waist as I was carried like a baby out of the club . . . super glamorous, I know!)

Back when I hit rock bottom and the doctor plonked the tray of medications in front of me and said I had to take them indefinitely, I knew that wasn't good enough or right for me. I felt the same about alcohol when I made the decision to quit in 2010. My intuition was telling me that it wasn't supporting me or my growth and it was time to stop. I needed to focus my attention on healing, self-love, and rebuilding my immune system, and alcohol was definitely not going to help with that. I decided to quit and concentrate all my energy on getting well and choosing love over fear. I didn't put a time frame on this new venture; I just decided it wasn't right for me in that moment. I was actually quite excited to experiment with it and see how it made me feel.

The first two months of quitting were the hardest. At the time it was coming into summer and there were parties, soirées, events, and dinners each week. Showing up to these celebrations and not drinking was really difficult—I felt like a fish out of water. It was like learning how to walk again. It brought up all my Mean Girl insecurities and I didn't really know how to be me. People would ask me why I wasn't drinking, and I would always come up with an awkward response because I was scared of being judged. I wasn't yet confident in my decision or in myself, and I cared way too much what others thought of me. What I really wanted to reply was, "Because I just don't feel like it." But of course, I didn't.

These days, not only does no one else care, but I don't care what other people think. I have learned to flex my self-love muscle and be comfortable in my own skin. I don't care what anyone else thinks—especially about something as minor as whether I drink. To be honest, most of the people around me now rarely drink. Occasionally they'll have a glass of red wine, but no one is binge drinking, that's for sure. They all honor their temples too much.

Choosing not to drink alcohol seems to be a topic that triggers a lot of questions. Here are some of the ones I get asked the most.

Do you miss drinking? Absolutely not!

Will you ever drink again? Who knows? It's been years and right now, at this point in my life, it's not for me. It doesn't serve me and it stops me from feeling fabulously healthy.

How do you feel? Abso-freaking-lutely amazing!

Has it affected your relationships? It has. My entire circle of friends has shifted since those pre-rock-bottom days.

Do you feel like you are missing out? No way in hell! One of the things I loved about going out was busting some serious moves on the D floor, which I still do—just sans alcohol. Or I do it in my lounge room with my boys and the music (usually One Direction: again, don't judge me) blaring.

Do you ever feel peer pressure? Not at all. However, I definitely did at the start. But once you start to flex your self-love muscle, it's smooth sailing.

Does your hubby drink? Nope. He also loves his temple too much.

There are so many awesome benefits you will feel from quitting drinking, including having more energy, clearer skin, brighter eyes, and less stress. Another unexpected bonus was that I lost all the cellulite on my thighs once I stopped drinking. Pretty cool, huh?

A few years ago, I gave my dad—who's very Italian, by the way, and loves a glass (or three) of red every night with dinner—the challenge of giving up alcohol for one month. He lost fifteen pounds without changing anything else in his diet or lifestyle. He said he had never had so much energy and clarity and he now looks at alcohol very differently.

Another amazing benefit of quitting drinking was how clear and focused I began to feel. I am so much more productive these days. I especially enjoy my Sundays—feeling energized and not hungover is a huge change! In the past, Sundays were a write-off. Now I feel like I have a whole extra day in my week. It's awesome!

I couldn't imagine ever going back to that way of living where I was trashing my body all the time. Giving up drinking has been one of the absolute best choices for me. But, just like everything else in this book, do what's right for you. Tune in to yourself and next time you're out, ask yourself, "Do I actually really feel like a drink tonight?" If the answer is no, then don't do it. Honor yourself enough to say a firm but loving no to others and a radiant yes to your heart. This is a true act of self-love.

And if you do feel like having a glass of something, make sure it's the best quality you can find, then go for it! Enjoy it, let go of the guilt, and don't let your Mean Girl beat you up for it—I believe the guilt is far more harmful than the actual drink itself. So if you are going to have a drink, then do it with total love and enjoyment.

Inspo-action

Are you up for a little challenge? If you have never quit the bottle, I encourage you to give it a go for twenty-one days and see how you feel. Have an open mind and do it as an experiment. If you never try it, you will never know how radiant you can truly feel.

Have fun with it and instead of going out drinking on a Saturday night, invite your soul sisters over for a goddess night where you share healthy food, read angel cards, and dance around your lounge room. Sounds cheesy, but it's loads of fun!

> **Some other things you can do instead of going out drinking include . . .**
>
> ↪ Hosting a dinner party or a potluck where everyone brings a dish to share.
>
> ↪ Seeing a movie.
>
> ↪ Heading to a play or musical.
>
> ↪ Going to see some live music.
>
> ↪ Holding a board-game night at your home.
>
> ↪ Staying in and jumping in the bath with a good book.
>
> ↪ Going to bed at eight thirty p.m. (how's that for a novel idea?).

Exercise with Heart

Movement is the other key element of feeling fabulously healthy.

I used to exercise out of fear of getting fat. I have never been seriously overweight, but I would flog my body daily with Victoria's Secret models in the forefront of my mind out of fear and hatred of what I saw in the mirror. After I burned myself out with fatigue and adrenal exhaustion, I realized that exercising was yet another opportunity to choose love. Now I move my body in a loving way each day. No more pushing, flogging, and trying to whip my body into shape with fear in my mind. I love and accept myself unconditionally, and I move because I love the way it makes me feel. Not because I hate my body and want to fix and change it. There's a big difference.

Things are always going to be harder when you come from fear. Life will flow a lot more effortlessly when you come from love.

Be honest with yourself now and ask yourself, "Am I exercising because I freakin' love the way it makes me feel? Or am I doing it because I hate the size of my thighs and want them to be smaller?"

It's important to remember that if you want love to be the default setting on your internal GPS, you have to do everything out of love. Even exercise.

Inspo-action

Start to move your body out of love and notice the difference in how you feel. Find things you enjoy and do them consistently. Take a moment right now to schedule in your digital calendar when you are going to lovingly move your body so that there is no room for your Mean Girl to make excuses. (Seriously, go do it—I'll wait!)

Now write down five different ways you love to move your body.

_____

_____

_____

_____

_____

Remember, consistency counts! It's the little things you do each day that add up to big results or big consequences.

BUT WHY SHOULD I EXERCISE?

Here are my top ten reasons you need to move your body . . .

1. *It keeps you young and adds years to your life.*

   Exercise keeps you young at a cellular level and helps to ward off the degenerative effects of aging. Research shows that exercise might even trump genes when it comes to staying youthful and healthy.

2. *It boosts your confidence.*

   Even if you aren't seeing results straightaway, the mental effect working out has on you will boost your confidence and make you feel good. (And remember, feeling good is what it's all about.)

3. *It reduces stress and anxiety.*

   Stress wreaks havoc on your body and health. It depletes your immune system and mucks up your hormones. Regular exercise can decrease your overall stress both mentally and physically.

4. *It boosts creativity.*

   Research shows that regular exercisers fare better on creativity tests than nonexercisers. On a personal note, I often get my best ideas when I'm out walking in the park or swimming in the ocean.

5. *It improves your sleep.*

Regular exercise can even make you sleep better (although exercising just before bed isn't a good idea, because it can be too stimulating).

6. *It gives you more energy.*

If you are someone who struggles with low energy, you might be wondering how on earth expending more energy by exercising can make you feel better. But it does! In fact, the rush of endorphins from a good workout session can't be beat! It's also a great afternoon pick-me-up. Instead of reaching for that three p.m. coffee or chocolate bar, do some exercise instead. Even a purposeful-looking walk around the building or getting some paper for the photocopier will suffice.

7. *It boosts your immune system and protects against disease.*

Moving your body can help keep you well and help fight off any nasty bugs and germs. Research shows that people who regularly exercise get fewer colds and flus than those who don't. (However, be careful not to overdo it—overtraining can make you more susceptible to illness. Make sure you're always listening to your body.)

8. *It improves your sex life.*

Exercise increases your cardiovascular endurance, muscular strength, and flexibility—all of which enhance your sex life. It also improves circulation (which is pretty important when it comes to sexy-time!).

9. *It helps you kick those sugar cravings.*

Daily exercise helps maintain a healthy blood-sugar level by increasing the cells' sensitivity to insulin and by controlling weight. A sweet bonus indeed!

10. *It gives you better focus.*

Regular exercise has been shown to improve mental focus, enhance memory, and decrease the dreaded "brain fog."

Not too shabby results for simply getting your bum moving, huh? All you need to do is start with thirty minutes every day to reap the benefits. Think of it as an act of self-love.

How to Fall in Love with Exercise

These days, I love exercise so much that it's a nonnegotiable part of my daily routine. But it wasn't always like that, and I know how tough it can be when you're starting out. Here are my favorite ways to fall in love with movement and get the most out of your workouts:

౼ Find something you enjoy.

Whether it's boxing, yoga, soft-sand running, Nia dance, barre, weights, Pilates, competitive sports, walking, swimming, paddle-boarding, dancing, whatever . . . it really doesn't matter what form of movement it is, as long as you are having fun and getting your heart rate up each day.

- Mix it up.

     I have a friend who has done the same aerobics classes
for almost eighteen years and wonders why she doesn't
get results. Of course, any exercise is good for you, but your
body likes diversity. It needs to be "surprised" by doing
different activities to keep it guessing and growing.

- Train with your bestie.

     I love exercising with my besties; you get to catch up
and do a workout—double whammy of goodness! However,
it's always good to plan a little catch-up either before or
after your workout. That way you won't talk the entire way
through the session . . . (guilty!).

- Work out from love, not fear.

     I used to slog it out on the treadmill for an hour because
I hated what I saw in the mirror—totally a fear-based way
of operating. Now I work out because I love the way it
makes me feel.

- Don't think you need to always be pushing your body to
exhaustion.

     Gentle, nurturing movements like walking are great for
your body and mind. I love holistic whole-body movements
like yoga, Pilates, and barre. I also love incidental exercise
like playing cricket in the park with Leo.

- Utilize the power of music.

     Create kick-arse playlists to enhance your workouts—a
high-energy one for when you feel like getting your heart
pumping and a softer, more gentle one for your walks in
nature and yoga practice.

ↁↁ Quit listening to your Mean Girl.

Know that the voice that says, "I can't go any farther!" or "I can't hold a plank pose for two minutes!" is just your Mean Girl. Our bodies are amazing and are capable of awesome things. So be aware of when your Mean Girl tries to tell you otherwise.

Inspo-action

Struggling to make time for exercise? You must schedule it in your calendar if you want to get it done. As you know, I love digital calendars, because I can color code the different areas of my life. I have my workout sessions in yellow, which repeats every day at six a.m. That way, my Mean Girl can't provide sneaky reasons not to do it.

Now, there are going to be times when stuff comes up. That's okay. However, scheduling it in your calendar sets you up for success and makes it so much more likely to happen. We are creatures of habit, so if you book it in at the same time each day you're more likely to make it happen, plus you take out the thinking process. If you don't schedule it you're likely to let it slide today, then tomorrow and the next day. Before you know it, three months have gone by without a single session. So if you didn't do it before, pop it in your calendar now! Your body and mind will thank you.

Don't Shoot the Messenger

Given half the chance and the right internal and external environment, our bodies have an innate ability to heal and regenerate. We have an incredible built-in ecosystem that knows how to repair, recover, and rebuild itself. But, of course, if we're not treating our bodies with love, these amazing functions don't work at their peak, and we start breaking down and getting sick. When that started happening to me, I was so hard on myself. I would get so angry and resentful toward my body, and I felt so frustrated that it was letting me down . . . a perfect stage for my Mean Girl.

I was also so fearful of getting adrenal fatigue again and not fully healing that I continued to attract that into my life. It wasn't until I reprogrammed my way of thinking that I slowly started to feel vital and well again.

Our bodies are always trying to talk to us. They are constantly giving us gentle reminders to rebalance. When we ignore those gentle nudges for long enough, it can manifest as an illness or disease. I used to ignore the signs for days, if not weeks, until I would land in the doctor's office or emergency department. If only I'd looked after myself when I first felt a niggle, I could have avoided a whole lot of pain and suffering, not to mention the money and time it cost me.

Our job, as the proud owners and operators of these amazing bodies we've been given for this time here on earth, is to check in with them regularly and respond to their needs.

A few weeks ago, I was feeling a little under the weather—nothing serious, but just not as healthy, strong, and vibrant as I usually feel. So . . . I stayed in bed. Yes, I had loads to do, meetings to attend, a book to finish, school drop-off, and my team counting on me. But in that moment, what I needed most of all was to flex my self-love muscle and ask, "What is going to most serve me right now?" The answer was clear: to rest. Which is exactly what I did. I spent the whole morning in bed, and by the afternoon I was feeling back to normal and was able to go into the office. I understand that not everyone can take the morning off, and in that case you could perhaps talk to your manager at work about swapping to a quieter position for that shift. Or you could get a friend to carpool your kids and say you'll do it later in the week. All I know is if I hadn't taken that time out to recoup, I could still be paying the price now a few weeks later. But I listened to my body. It was sending me warning signs, so I took note and changed my course. In a society where we are constantly told to "pull your socks up" and "keep charging forward no matter the cost," I've had to consciously choose to unlearn those attitudes because that is not the model I want to subscribe to.

Soul Share

There is always a price to pay when you don't listen to your messenger. The body never lies. Act accordingly.

Next time you feel a niggle, check in with yourself and do whatever you need to do to rebalance. If you can take the morning off, do so: meditate, have a bath, nourish your temple, whatever you've got to do. You'll thank yourself for it later.

Mental Health Check

Now that you have all the tools to nourish your body from the outside in, let's chat about mental health. And when I say mental health, I am referring to Mean Girl mind chatter—not serious mental illnesses. Because you now know that being fabulously healthy isn't just about what you put in your body and how you move, it's also about what's going on upstairs with your Mean Girl.

Becoming aware of the Mean Girl thoughts in your head is just as important as what you put into your mouth.

My belief is when you are in the present moment there are no thoughts, just pure presence! You can't be present and thinking at the same time—it's impossible. So ideally let's be in the here and now; then there are no thoughts. However, most of us spend way too much time upstairs in thought—and Mean Girl thoughts at that. So if you are going to have thoughts let's keep 'em nice and clean. No more Mean Girl nasty comments that keep you stuck in Fear Town. Deal?

Be mindful of other people's thoughts and energy too. Most people will want to dump their baggage on you and bring you down to their level.

EVERYONE IS ALWAYS SEEKING UNITY

You know those times at work when someone is bitching about someone else and it makes you feel kind of uncomfortable? Don't feel like you have to join in to be polite. Remember, that person is simply seeking unity and it's an opportunity for you to rise up. Instead of being brought to their level, you could change the subject by giving that person an authentic compliment such as, "I really like that color blue on you; it brings out your eyes." That's a great way to disarm a bitching session that you don't want to take part in.

Gossip is highly toxic, and every time you say something nasty or negative about someone else you are diminishing your aura and strengthening theirs. Do not engage in any sort of gossip or bitch session. Your Mean Girl will try to get you involved but don't let her.

Try these ideas next time you find yourself in the middle of a gossip sesh:

- Quickly excuse yourself to the bathroom.
- Change the subject by paying that person an authentic compliment.
- And if you really want to step up and stand in your truth, simply say something like, "Mary isn't here to defend herself so I don't think we should talk about her."

Inspo-action

Think about a time this week when you have said something nasty about someone else. How did it make you feel? Icky, heavy, gross? Take a moment to write it down.

_____

_____

Committing to banishing gossip and bitch sessions from your life will create more space for magic and miracles to flow to you.

And remember, if you entertain crappy thoughts, you are going to feel crappy—it's that simple.

Let's aim for presence as our first option. Second option is awesome thoughts (if we are going to think), and the third option is Mean Girl nasty thoughts . . . I know which one I choose.

Being Fabulously Healthy Recap

- How you treat your body is a direct reflection of how you feel about yourself.
- Consciously choose this affirmation: "I love and accept myself unconditionally and move my body because I love the way it makes me feel."
- Choose love, because you always get what you fear most.
- There's always a price to pay when you don't listen to your body.
- Remember, consistency matters. It's the little things you do each day that add up to big results or big consequences.
- Presence is key for mental health.

FIVE

Let passion pump your pulse

Don't get so busy making a living that you
forget to make a life.

DOLLY PARTON

I believe we are here to do what we love and to share our unique gifts with the world. I also believe no one is more special than anyone else and doing what you love isn't reserved for someone smarter, prettier, wealthier, or "better" than you—it's absolutely your prerogative too. I also believe that we are not here to be a slave to a desk, office, or job we loathe . . . What's the point in that?! We are here to discover what we are truly passionate about and let that become the life-force that pumps through our veins.

Now that I know all this, I don't think I could ever do something I wasn't passionate about. Your work is not who are you, but it is something you spend a lot of time doing—so why not do something that lights you up and puts profits in your pockets at the same time?

I've had two careers in my lifetime, both driven by passion.

When I first started as a performer I loved what I did so much that it never felt like work. Similarly to now: speaking, writing, and creating products to inspire women to be wildly wealthy, fabulously healthy, and bursting with love doesn't feel like work to me. And I feel deeply grateful I have had these two careers that made my heart sing.

Although let it be said, there were definitely a few years in between where I got lost. I took any job just to make money—working in retail, nannying three children under the age of six (not easy), working as a promo girl handing out flyers on the streets, being the door girl for different clubs, dancing in nightclubs, and working in admin. Now, there is nothing wrong with those jobs, but they didn't light me up and I was doing them for the wrong reason—just to make money. At that time I didn't really know my worth. However, I soon realized that I could find my passion again: I just needed to do some inner work. Fortunately I found my way again and got back on my true path.

In my experience, life doesn't get much better than doing what you love each day and helping others in the process. But I know that a lot of my clients think that it's not possible for them to make a living doing what they enjoy. They think that they just have to grit their teeth, hold their tongue, and plod through their forty-hour work weeks doing something that they don't even like, let alone love. But let me tell you something: you can do work you love. It truly is possible. If you're feeling resistance to this idea, or are struggling to believe that you could ever do what you love, it's likely because of one of these reasons:

1. Your Mean Girl is telling you that you can't make money from your passion.

2. Your Mean Girl is trying to keep you small and stuck inside your comfort zone (by telling you your business idea will never work, that you'll never get promoted, that you shouldn't bother going for that new job, that you could never write a book . . .).

3. Your worthy-o-meter is too low and you don't believe you are worthy of doing something that pumps passion through your veins each day.

Which one resonates with you?

It's also important to mention that I am well aware that some people don't necessarily love their work but aren't willing to make any shifts and that's totally fine also. Everyone is different and you need to do what's right for you, always! But if that's the case I want to encourage you to find the love in your work, find the joy and gratitude for actually having a job that provides you with income to put a roof over your head and food on the table. Or the fact that you actually have a job to go to and nice people (or even one nice person) to work with. Whatever it is, find that joy and gratitude; otherwise, it will feel like a hard slog.

There are two choices with everything in life: you can either change it or accept it, which means you've got to quit whining about it.

There are so many successful people out there making a living out of their passion—from accountants to Zen meditation teachers, from entrepreneurs to electricians. There are also heaps of people in jobs they hate out of fear of following their heart. So which one are you?

If you are the latter, let's put that to bed, once and for all. Let's dial up your worthy-o-meter and really get things crankin'. The time to live your dream life is *now*—don't put it off for another second!

Inspo-action

What is one thing you can do right now to edge you a tiny bit closer to your dream career? Can you phone someone? Request an introduction? Send off a proposal? Write a book outline? Register a business name? The career of your dreams starts with one tiny step, so identify one you can put into action *today*.

_____

_____

_____

_____

Every second is a precious gift you will never get back.
Don't waste it.

How to Find Your Passion

Working as a life, health, and business coach for many years, the most common thing I would get asked by my clients—more than anything else—was . . . How do I know what my passion is? How do I figure out my life's purpose?

Yep, passion trumps everything else. It seems to be the thing we are most searching for and are the most desperate to find. People go to extreme lengths to try to figure it out—traveling across continents, doing endless courses and training programs, consulting counselors, psychics, and shamans. But it doesn't have to be that complex (or expensive).

You see, your passion is already within you; it always has been! You don't need to go out shopping, looking, or searching for it; it's there inside your heart. You just haven't accessed it for a while. You simply need to get it down from the top shelf where you've stored it, dust off the cobwebs, and get reacquainted.

Inspo-action

Ready to dive deep and figure out your true passion? Grab your pen and get riffing on the following questions. Don't judge what comes to the surface, and don't censor yourself. Simply let it pour onto the page. Ready?

✍ What lights you up from your core?

_____

_____

_____

✍ What do you lose hours doing?

_____

_____

_____

✍ What would you do for free?

_____

_____

_____

✑ What inspires you to jump out of bed each
morning?

_____

_____

_____

There's your passion, beautiful.

WHAT IF I HAVE TOO MANY PASSIONS?

If you're someone who's got lots of things you're equally passionate about, it can seem massively overwhelming to try to narrow it down to just one focus.

But here's the good news: you don't have to!

Being multipassionate rocks. I am passionate about loads of things—writing, speaking, yoga, inspiring people, being of service, entrepreneurship, wellness, meditation, living a toxin-free life, creating kick-arse online programs, travel and adventure, nature, protecting the environment, living every moment to the fullest, Leo, walking hand in hand through life with my darling husband, love, health, and abundance . . . to name a few!

Just because you have a few things that inspire the heck out of you, doesn't mean you have to pick one and forget about all the rest. It just means you have to start with one and build from there. Start with the one thing you can see yourself making a career out of. That thing that really lights you up from your core and would inspire you to jump out of bed each day.

Now that you are flowing, notice if your Mean Girl has popped up. When we start talking about our passions and things that light us up, she will come knocking. Be mindful of her sneaky ways, gently close the door on her, and stay connected to that feeling you get when you think about your passions.

Many years ago, I started out with a passion for health and wellness. I built a business with that as my focus, without fully understanding how the rest of my passions would come into play. Years later that simple premise has led me where I am today—speaking and running epic live events around the world, writing this book with my dream publishers, inspiring a global tribe of women, creating life-changing online programs, and helping people to live their best lives. There is no way in the world I could have predicted what has transpired. It is beyond my wildest dreams. It all started with a passion for health and wellness and it has grown from there. So don't try to get ahead of yourself and "logically" work it all out. Just keep following your heart and trust that you are Universally supported and the rest will unfold in perfect time.

Still not sure where to start? If you have a few things that you love, ask yourself, "What am I most drawn to?" What one thing makes you want to scream, *"Hell yeah!"* from the top of the mountains?

There's your answer. That's where you start. Don't let your Mean Girl sabotage you with questions like "How is it all going to work?" Or "How will I make money from it?" Just stay connected with that *hell yeah* feeling you get when you think about your passion and the rest will unfold as it's supposed to. Your Mean Girl will try to stop you from following your heart by planting these fears in your mind. Your job is not to let her win.

Remember, you are always supported when you follow your heart.

I grew up watching both my parents do something they loved for work. My mum is a midwife and nurse, while my dad owns a few businesses, one being an air-conditioning company. They both love their work. Dad was actually telling me over dinner the other night that he doesn't think he will ever retire. I asked him why and he responded, "Why would I? I love what I do." Point taken! That's the place you want to get to—where you would do it forever just because you love it. I feel the same about my work: I can't imagine ever stopping writing and teaching.

Because my parents both followed their hearts, my family didn't think it was strange when I decided to pack up all my worldly belongings and do the same. After high school, when I announced that I was moving to another city to go to performing arts college, they told me to go for it. They have always encouraged me to follow my dreams and do what my heart desires. I am forever grateful for that.

Not everyone grows up in such an open, supportive environment: I get that. My friend Steph was expected to go to university to study law regardless of her own passions, because that was what everyone else in her family had done. Despite being incredibly talented and wanting to start her own jewelry business, she toed the line and is still a lawyer, eight years down the track. (She still hopes to follow her heart and start that jewelry studio . . . one day.)

My client Monica never even realized that following her heart was an option. She watched her parents go to jobs they loathed their entire lives, then retire unsatisfied and remain miserable and directionless throughout their "golden years." She'd heard her parents say over and over again that life was tough, that you had to suck it up, grit your teeth, and bear it, and that the world was against them. They were always playing the victim and pulling the "poor me" card, constantly deflecting any responsibility for the way their life was unfolding. That sort of programming sinks in deep, without us even realizing. As a result, when she left school, she followed in her parents' footsteps, getting an average-but-safe job that she hated and didn't light her up. Again, that's okay if that's your truth, but own it and stop complaining about it.

I am telling you this because awareness is key. If you grew up having an experience similar to Steph's and Monica's, I want to remind you that you don't have to reenact the same scenario as the people around you. You truly can walk your own path and blaze your own trail. Now that you are aware of it, it's up to you to take action. And whether that's pursuing your passion as your career, pursuing your passion outside of office hours, or being in a job you don't necessarily love but finding the joy and gratitude within it anyway . . . whatever it is, take action now.

Inspo-action

🖎 What attitudes about work did your parents instill in you?

_____

_____

_____

↙ What attitudes about work do you want to
consciously take with you moving forward?

_____

_____

_____

Passion Drives Your Purpose

When you are authentically living a passion-fueled life and doing
what you love, you are automatically aligned to your purpose and
mission in the world.

Inspo-action

Articulating your mission out loud can be a very powerful exercise—it helps you home in on what is most important to you and how you most want to make an
impact on this planet. Like I mentioned before, my mission in life is to inspire women to become wildly wealthy,
fabulously healthy, and bursting with love. This lights me
up and puts a fire in my belly. That's what your mission is
supposed to do.

What's your mission?

_____

_____

_____

There will be things, people, and events in your life that will make you detour off your true path. Your job is to keep your mission at the forefront of your mind, so that you are always aligned and "on purpose"; otherwise, you will constantly be distracted and nothing will ever get done. Use your mission to help guide you back to your truth.

Distractions and detours are things you have to get skilled at dealing with. I often get e-mails asking me to speak at different events, do interviews, or represent various brands or companies. The first question I ask myself is, "Is it aligned to my mission and part of my purpose?" If the answer is yes, then I move forward wholeheartedly. If the answer is no, then I graciously decline. In the earlier stages of my career, I found it much harder to say no. I took on everything that came my way—I was eager, excited, and not crystal clear on my mission. As a result, I never got much done. I was constantly distracted, fulfilling other people's desires and not staying true to my own.

Every time an opportunity presents itself to you, whether it's a business venture, an event invite, or a holiday with friends, ask yourself if it's aligned with your purpose and mission in the world. This simple question will help keep you on track and on purpose.

Honor your time and know that you don't have to say yes to every single opportunity that presents itself to you. We live in a world where FOMO (fear of missing out) is all too common and our Mean Girl undermines us on the pretense of looking after others. But what about letting yourself down: does that not matter? These are the moments when you need to tune in, flex your self-love muscle, and do what feels right for you. Your mission matters, so it's time to stop fulfilling everyone else's expectations and let your passion drive your purpose.

Creativity and Passion

We are all creative beings, and we all have the capacity to express our creativity freely. As children we are incredibly creative: building forts, painting masterpieces, and creating Lego landscapes like nobody's business. However, as we grow we lose that sense of play, exploration, and creativity, because life gets "serious and hard," and because some people let their Mean Girl tell them they aren't creative. But that belief is BS, and it could actually be a massive block for you. When creativity is not expressed, it lies dormant, festering in our bodies and eating away at our souls. Sometimes it manifests as an illness or disease, sometimes as anger or frustration. And until you find a way to express it and channel that energy into the world, it will keep building up. That's why it's important to nurture your creativity and do something each day that allows you to express yourself freely. For me, my biggest creative outlet is writing—this is where I let my creative juices flow. But I also have dance-offs in my husband's music studio, get creative in the kitchen with nourishing food, do yoga, walk in nature, lie on my balcony and marvel at the shapes of the clouds, build Legos with Leo, paint, and pretend I am Beyoncé in the car. All these things stretch my creativity and give me a sense of play.

Inspo-action

How can you add more play and creativity to your life?
Write down five ideas.

_____

_____

_____

_____

_____

No matter what your passion or mission in life, there will always be some element of creativity inside you that wants to be expressed. If you're an accountant, get creative with the design of your spreadsheets. If you work in the corporate world, pretend you're speaking on the TED stage when you give your next presentation. If you're a hairdresser, imagine you are Michelangelo sculpting your latest masterpiece as you put the finishing touches on a client's blowout. Have fun with it, and remember that the more you play and flex your creative muscles, the easier it is and the more creative you become.

Creativity is the crux of your passion.

Inspo-action

Commit to doing one thing each day that gets your creative juices flowing. Add it into your calendar right now.

Never "Work" Again

Do you want to never work another day in your life? Then let out your passion and start to live it.

What I do for a living definitely doesn't feel like work—I love it! I jump out of bed each morning with fist-pumping enthusiasm; I can't wait to get to my office and sink my teeth into the day's tasks. I would even do it for free—heck, there are still things I do do for free, simply because I love them so much and they're beautifully aligned with my mission. Remember, darling, I am a normal gal just like you and you can live your passion also. You just have to make a choice, turn up your worthy-o-meter, and let go of your Mean Girl thoughts. If I can do it, so can you!

You will never work another day of your life if passion is what's pumping your pulse.

My husband spent seven years in a very successful band called Sneaky Sound System. He traveled the world and passion was definitely swimming through his veins—music is his lifeblood. However, he then decided to do something more "stable," so he went and got a "real job" as a high-end real estate agent selling some of the most expensive properties in Australia. Although he was extremely successful at it—he even won an award as Australia's top sales agent of 2009—and did it for many years, it wasn't his truth. And deep down, he knew it. That inner discord meant that it was only a matter of time before something had to give. Eventually, he fell very ill with meningitis, fibromyalgia, chronic fatigue, and a whole host of other health issues. Like me, he ended up in hospital, and he took three years to recover. Yep, three years.

During that time, he didn't work; he focused all his energy on healing. Toward the end of his three years, he got back into doing things that inspired him. In the years that followed, he created an online meditation program, created and launched a leading digital magazine for entrepreneurs, started producing a high-budget feature film called *Superhuman*, created a health app, worked in my business, and launched his soul music career. Although these career choices were a lot more aligned with his truth, the mix still wasn't one hundred percent him. There was no getting around his truth—my husband's passion and mission in life is to reconnect people with their hearts through his music. Now that he has embraced his passion and is making music full-time, he is in his element and things are flowing a whole lot more effortlessly. It's incredible to watch. And I tell you what, there is nothing sexier than a man who is true to his mission and purpose in life.

When you are doing what you love, it won't feel like work. It is an expression of you, something you love and get paid for.

So, let me ask you this, beautiful: are you making a life or a living? Look at the people who inspire you—whether it's Tony Robbins, Steve Jobs, Richard Branson, Ellen DeGeneres, Oprah Winfrey, J. K. Rowling, or Deepak Chopra. All these people started with a simple passion . . . and look where it has gotten them today!

Don't try to figure out all the details now, don't get bogged down in the nuts and bolts, and don't invent a million reasons why you can't follow your passion—that's just your Mean Girl trying to stop you from following your dreams. Let go of the "how" and stay connected to the feeling you get when you think about your passion and mission. This is how you will never "work" again.

The Big Why

Once you know your passion and mission in life and you're ready to start living it, it's very important to get shiny-diamond clear on your "why," for both your business and your personal life. The idea in life is to wake up inspired and go to bed fulfilled and when you hold your why at the forefront of your mind it allows you to stay on your path and make it happen.

Consider Toms shoes. For those of you who aren't aware, Toms is an amazing company that gives a pair of shoes to children in need for every pair of shoes you buy. So when you purchase from them you aren't just buying shoes, you are buying into their why. You are saying, *I believe in this cause; I believe in their why.*

My why is the same as my mission: to inspire women to become wildly wealthy, fabulously healthy, and bursting with love. This is the reason behind everything I do—every word I write, every product I create, and every word I speak. It's the motivation that gets me out of bed each morning.

For me, I do what I do because I have no choice in the matter: I simply have to help, support, and inspire women! It's what makes my heart sing, it's how I most love to serve people, and I truly believe it's what I came here to do. This is why I am here. It's my calling and I wholeheartedly believe I was put on this planet to support and inspire women to be the best versions of themselves and to live their dream lives.

This is my why.

If you're still struggling to nail down the why behind your vision, tune in to your body. It always knows when you're aligned with your truth. Thinking about the reasons behind my mission gives me goose bumps, even after pursuing it for years—that's how you know you're on the right track!

Inspo-action

◈ Now let's think about your why: why do you do what you do?

_____

_____

_____

◈ Why do you have to do it?

_____

_____

_____

◈ Why does it light you up?

_____

_____

_____

Let's get your why into one powerful succinct sentence.

> ◎ My why is:
>
> _____
>
> _____
>
> Stick this on your fridge, vision board, computer, bathroom mirror, car dashboard . . . anywhere that you'll see it frequently and be reminded of it. Keeping it front and center of your mind is imperative—being continually connected to your why is crucial for staying on purpose. Feel free to share your why with your loved ones. Being on the same page as important people in your life is necessary and very helpful for keeping you on track for your mission.

Let Passion Pump Your Pulse Recap

◎ We came here to make a life, not a living.

◎ You are always supported when you follow your heart.

◎ If you're a multipassionate person, own it. However, home in on the one thing that excites you most.

◎ Remember, passion drives your purpose.

◎ Don't let your Mean Girl tell you that following your passion is not going to work or that you can't make money following your heart.

◎ Stay connected to your why. Have it at the forefront of your mind and everything you do.

Inspo-action

Now that you've got your passion and your why sorted, it's time to dial up your worthy-o-meter and really start to live it. No more sitting on the sidelines waiting for your time—your time is now!

🌙 What are three things that are stopping you from living your mission?

_____

_____

_____

Now it's time to get creative. Pick one of the above things, and have a little brainstorming session: what are five things you could do right now to sidestep, counteract, overcome, or completely love-bomb that obstacle out of the water?

I'll start you off with an example. Say you wanted to start a blog but were letting the fact that you don't know the technological stuff hold you back. To overcome that, you could:

🌙 Phone your cousin who works in IT and ask for his advice.

🌙 Find and watch a step-by-step YouTube tutorial walking you through the process.

- Shoot an e-mail to a blogger you admire and ask if they can recommend any resources.

- Pick up a few extra shifts at the restaurant you work at in order to pay a professional to do it for you.

- Offer to bake your tech-savvy bestie a delicious slow-cooked dinner if she'll spend a few hours holding your hand through the tough bits.

Your turn. Pick your obstacle and . . . go!

_____

_____

_____

_____

_____

(Super-duper bonus brownie points if you go through this process for each of the obstacles you identified.)

Now it's time to hold yourself accountable. You've got a list of achievable actions: now you simply need to start doing them. Remember, beautiful, you are so worthy of living your dream life: all it takes is some serious action right now.

SIX

being wildly wealthy

Happiness lies not in the mere possession
of money; it lies in the joy of achievement,
in the thrill of creative effort.

FRANKLIN D. ROOSEVELT

Let's talk about money, gorgeous.

How is your relationship with money right now?

Be really honest with yourself. Does the mere thought of money make you expand or contract? Do you constantly feel like you don't have enough? Or maybe you're frivolous, spending big-time and letting it slip all too easily through your fingers?

Be really honest with yourself and write it down:

I, _____, am very _____ with money.

For Old Melissa, mine would have said something like this:

I, Melissa, am very tight with money. I believe money is hard to come by, which comes from a place of fear.

Now mine would say something like this:

I, Melissa, am very neutral with money. I no longer put power in money. I believe money will always show up for that which is true for me.

As you can see, I used to have a very unhealthy relationship with money. I was convinced that there wasn't enough to go around, and that if I wasn't careful, I would run out and end up with nothing. Hello, scarcity mentality! So from the age of fourteen, I scrimped and saved every cent I could. And though my bank balance slowly began to grow, I hung on to those dollars with a white-knuckled grip and acted completely stingily. I was so focused on all that saving (out of fear) that I didn't live my life. The worst part was that my raging scarcity mentality leached out into all the other areas of my life.

The thing is, I wasn't born with this scarcity mentality. As I've said, we are born into this world as perfect, whole little beings. Like every belief, it was something I learned and picked up along the way. But from where?

Both my parents came from not a lot of money. They worked incredibly hard to allow my brother, sister, and me to have more opportunities. My dad migrated to Australia from Italy when he was six years old and couldn't speak a word of English. He worked really hard to learn the language and left school at fifteen to start working so he could contribute financially to his family.

My mum studied midwifery and nursing. At age twenty, she was knee-deep in her studies when she fell pregnant with my sister. She completed her final exams just months after giving birth. Until my sister was three years old, they all lived with my nonna in her two-bedroom, seventy-square-meter home, until they could afford to move out on their own.

Both my parents worked their bums off. Wholeheartedly and selflessly. I credit my drive to them.

So, how did this background affect my relationship with money?

Deep down, underneath all their hustling and hard work, my parents were scared that they would not have enough money and would not be able to provide for us kids. Unconsciously, I felt this fear and took it on myself. It became hardwired in my DNA, embedded in the way I viewed money. So all my life, I carried around their belief that I too might run out of money at any moment and not have enough to survive. It was like my GPS system was out of whack.

I don't blame my parents for this programming: they were doing the very best they could with the knowledge and understanding they had at the time. But I do want to point out that whatever you don't heal within yourself, you pass right on down to your children. Something to be mindful of.

Regarding my money beliefs, things changed only after my big crash-and-burn. I had started my inward journey and was well on my path to wellness when I became aware that my underlying beliefs affected everything from my health to my relationships and my emotions . . . It occurred to me that maybe I had some less-than-great beliefs around money too. When I took a big breath and started to go inward, I realized that the attitudes I had weren't actually my truth. I was carrying around their fear, something I see so commonly among my clients and friends.

So what was my truth? What was right for me? When I sat with it, and sought the answer from that deep-down place inside, a totally different philosophy bubbled up:

- I believe we are abundant beings and can create whatever our hearts desire.
- I believe that money will show up for that which is true for each of us.
- I believe we are limited only by our Mean Girl.
- I believe money is just energy that we use in exchange for something we value.
- I believe money should make you expand, not contract and close off.

This was what rang true for me. This was what I actually believed deep in my bones. But simply realizing it wasn't enough. I had to reprogram my money mind-set in the same way that I had reprogrammed my beliefs on health and love.

So I began to consciously embrace these heart-fueled truths. Every time my Mean Girl would rear her head and plant a limiting thought—*You can't afford that; you don't deserve wealth; you'll never have as much as so-and-so has*—I had to stop her, gently close the door on her, return to my heart, and let it go. It's hard work when you've had years of conditioning deeply ingrained into you. But it does get easier (I promise), and the more you practice catching those limiting beliefs in their tracks, the easier it becomes. Just like everything else, it's a metaphorical muscle that gets strengthened with use. Your job is to strengthen it daily.

You see, the truth is, like everything, your relationship with money is a reflection of all the other areas in your life. It's a great barometer for how you're going as a whole. So if you have a scarcity mentality regarding your finances, you'll more than likely have that same mentality in other areas of your life too, like your health and love.

And if you're someone who just ignores their money, and tries to bury their head in the sand, that's likely the same way you're approaching your health, relationships, and career too.

Inspo-action

So let's dig deep here . . .

What are your beliefs around money right now?

_____

_____

_____

Now let's get super honest: are these beliefs even yours, or are they someone else's—like your parents', partner's, or schoolteachers'?

If it's not your belief, then what do you believe in? What is your truth? What are your money beliefs?

When it comes to money, I believe that . . .

_____

_____

_____

_____

_____

This can be a really great exercise to do with your partner as well, so that you each know where the other stands. With all the financial decisions that you have to make individually and together, it can be very difficult to grow as a couple if your views aren't aligned and you don't have a common goal.

If you're not in a relationship, make sure the next person you meet has money beliefs and values similar to yours; otherwise, you're getting yourself into a hard slog of arguments and compromise. Not everyone is going to have the same beliefs as yours, and that's okay, but when you are entering a relationship there has to be unity on all levels (more on that later), even regarding your finances.

Once you've unearthed your actual beliefs, I want you to stick them up on your fridge as a constant reminder to replace those lousy old Mean Girl patterns that no longer serve you. You can take it a step further too—call your partner out (lovingly) when he or she entertains old beliefs, and get him or her to do the same for you. (Although you must remember to always come from a space of love.)

One of my clients, Jane, came to me with a very fear-driven relationship with money. She placed all her self-worth in the possession of material objects and was convinced that the latest Chanel handbag was going to make her happy and fulfilled. After a little digging, we uncovered that her relationship with money was a reflection of her father's. She informed me that her father came from a very poor family. He studied hard and worked his way up the corporate ladder to become a successful CEO for a major organization. But along the way he got lost in his wealth, valuing only money, status, and material objects. This was where Jane's beliefs stemmed from, causing her to believe that if she didn't have fancy material objects like a nice car, designer bag, and expensive shoes she wasn't (a) successful or (b) going to be accepted by her father.

When this realization hit her she broke down, but then she felt incredibly empowered that she could now let go of her father's beliefs around money and start to live out her own.

We must take action to break the cycle.

Once I shifted my relationship with money, things started to flow a whole lot more effortlessly for me. Suddenly, opportunities and abundance presented themselves in ways that I could never have imagined because I was finally open to them. And I want the same for you. But in order to find this ease and flow and become an abundance magnet, you first have to take the big, bold step of getting honest with yourself. Then with your partner too. Even though digging into this stuff may take you outside of your comfort zone, I promise you—the results will definitely be worth it. And remember, on the other side of your comfort zone is always growth.

If your partner (or anyone else, for that matter) tries to instill his or her financial beliefs into you, say a gentle thank-you for the input, then lovingly speak your truth. What's true for you (and your partner) is actually none of anyone else's business. (And remember this: opinions are like belly buttons; everybody's got one!)

The most important thing to remember throughout this whole journey to mastering your Mean Girl is to be truthful and honest with yourself. That's all that really matters. If you steer by your heart, you'll always be going in the right direction. Whenever you're in doubt, simply look within: that is where the answers are . . . always!

Money Is Energy

Thanks to the science of quantum physics, we know that everything in the Universe—including ourselves—is made up of waves and vibrating particles. Everything is energy—the book or device you are reading from right now, the chair you are sitting on, the walls that surround you. Matter is just energy that has been slowed down enough for it to take form and become visible to us. And money is no exception.

Many people believe money is bad, wrong, evil, or not "spiritual." This is not the case. Money is simply a unit of energetic exchange. At one time, people used cowrie shells as their unit of exchange and no one thought that was evil and wrong. It was simply something that people used in exchange for something else that had meaning and value to them.

Years ago, I received a free ticket to a personal-development workshop. The ticket would have cost me fifteen hundred dollars, and my Mean Girl was thrilled to have scored such a great freebie. I rocked up on the first morning (late), plonked my bum in my seat, was all prepared to soak up the goodness ... and then was surprised when I didn't actually get much out of the weekend at all. Later, I figured it out: it wasn't because of the workshop itself—it had been really great content (so everyone was telling me), presented by a brilliant speaker—but because there hadn't been a fair exchange of energy, I hadn't deeply valued what had been presented. As a result I didn't get anything out of the workshop.

Now I'm incredibly conscious of the importance of a fair energy exchange to ensure that I am truly valuing and honoring the energy that I'm receiving—whether that's a workshop, a beautiful meal, a massage, or anything.

Another example of this was when I first started dating my husband. He wanted to read my e-book *12 Steps to Wellness*, so I said I would e-mail it to him. He replied, "No, honey, I want to pay for it—I value you and your work, and I want to make that energetic exchange." He also mentioned that if he didn't pay for it he wouldn't value it as much.

There has to be an energetic exchange in order to truly value something.

I offered a free coaching session a few years ago as part of a competition. The girl who won rocked up on Skype fifteen minutes late, then she wasn't present and didn't really value my time or what was being offered. I guarantee if she had paid for that session she would have showed up very differently.

Think about a time in your life when you have been offered something for free and didn't truly value it. Now think about a time you have spent a lot of money on something (maybe it was a beautiful meal out) and truly savored every single second of the experience.

If there is no energetic exchange, you will not deeply value what you are receiving.

How do you view the exchange of money? Do you see it as evil, bad, unspiritual, and wrong? Or do you see it as just another form of sacred energy exchange?

Inspo-action

Practice an abundance mind-set. Every time you get a bill, don't think of it as a grudging obligation; instead, relabel your bills as expressions of appreciation. Feel grateful you can afford to have electricity, clean water, Internet, and a car. Every time a bill (even a parking fine) lands on my desk, I kiss the envelope and say, "Thank you." Putting that energy out into the Universe is much nicer than, "Oh crap, I can't afford this." Remember, you get back what you put out, so feel grateful you can make that exchange for something you value, like electricity.

Money itself isn't bad, no matter what we spend it on.

How people choose to use their money is up to them, and it's actually no one else's business. Some people may use their money toward things that others might feel is bad or wrong, but that doesn't mean that money itself is bad or wrong. There's a difference. Remember, there are also people out there using money for the greater good—building homes for the homeless, feeding the hungry, and healing the ill.

How are you using your money?

It's very important to get crystal clear on what you want to spend your money on. Is it aligned with your truth and core values in life? The answers to those questions can reveal a lot about your relationship with money.

In my early twenties, having a new outfit to wear every Saturday night, owning the latest designer handbag, and making my way through the cocktail menu at the hottest nightclub were high priorities. That was where my money went. Now it's very different. Every time I open my wallet, I check in with myself and ask, "Is this true for me? Do I really need this?" Asking these questions keeps me aligned with my core values, not only around money but also around my desire to tread lightly on this beautiful planet.

There are loads of opportunities to align your spending with your values, if you choose to look for them. Recently, my husband and I went out to dinner with a big group of friends and, at the end of the night, the suggestion was made that we split the bill evenly between all of us. Some people had had a fair few drinks—which is totally fine, but at this point in my life drinking alcohol is not my truth and it doesn't feel true for me to pay for the alcohol bill. Why would I pay for someone else to drink when I believe so strongly in treating my body like a temple? It just didn't make sense to me. I shared my view (gently, and with love) with the rest of the table, and, like true friends, they received it with love. "Great point," my friend Matt said.

Another example of how I align my spending with my values was at our wedding. My darling and I knew that we wanted the day to be a celebration of our beliefs as well as our love. Which meant that even if the price was higher, we chose products, services, and companies that were eco-friendly, organic, local, sustainable, and aligned with our core values, rather than taking the cheaper option. And boy, did standing in our truth feel good.

We also decided to have a dry wedding. It didn't feel true for us to supply alcohol to the people we love most. Instead, we had fresh coconuts with colorful funky straws on arrival, along with a super-food smoothie bar, a cold-pressed juice bar, kombucha on tap, and a cute herbal tea station. They were all organic, all a huge hit, and all aligned with our beliefs.

Just because something is common, that doesn't mean you have to follow it. Blaze your own trail and be a leader, not a follower. Every time you deny your truth and don't act in alignment there is always a consequence.

Take a look at your own spending habits. Is what you spend your money on aligned with your beliefs? Do you spend your cash on sweatshop clothing, fast food, and toxic products? Or do you take a moment before you whip out your wallet to make sure your purchases are aligned?

From now on, every time you hand over cash, check in with yourself and make sure the purchase is one hundred percent aligned with your core values and beliefs.

Giving Back

For many years I wanted to align myself with a charity I truly believed in. I researched organizations for depression and eating disorders, things that were close to my heart, but nothing jumped out at me. So I parked the idea and stopped pushing it; I knew I had planted the seed and the perfect organization would manifest in due course. Then in 2014, on our honeymoon, my husband and I were lying on the beach in Positano with our heads buried deep in our books when—tears streaming down my face—I turned to my husband and said, "Child sex slavery: I want to help save girls from sex slavery."

In 2011, Nick had raised funds to build a school in Kenya. And he said he would reach out to the people he did that through to see if there were any organizations they'd recommend I connect with. But we never heard back.

Months later, we were back home and saw a car with a bumper sticker that read "Destiny Rescue: Ending child sexual exploitation and slavery." Immediately I whipped out my phone and looked up the group. "This is it," I said to my husband. "This is the organization we've been waiting for." As soon as we got home, we e-mailed them, and we heard back right away. I met with one of the team members, Sue, and was blown away by the details I learned and by the mere fact that this tragedy still happens. As I sat, listening intently, heart breaking, I held back my tears as she shared how a rescue is performed. In that moment I knew I had to help.

I love this organization and love helping as much as I can.

Now, there are two reasons I am telling you this . . . First, when you find a cause you are truly passionate about, giving will not seem like an effort or a burden. In fact, you'll gladly open your heart (and wallet) as wide as you possibly can. And second, this is yet another example of why it's so important to stay true to *you* and your heart's desires. There are so many worthy causes in the world, and I truly believe that everyone can find the one that is right for them. You might be madly passionate about animal welfare, saving the environment, ending poverty, championing people who live with a disability, advocating for women's rights, solving homelessness, or something else entirely . . . It's beautiful to throw our weight behind those causes that truly light our heart-fire and speak to us on a soul level. I know I'm meant to be helping these kids, and I take pride and joy in doing so. Who are you being called to help?

One more thing: make sure that if you give to a charity or organization, you know exactly where your money is going. Unfortunately there are some people out there who behave unscrupulously around our generosity. I want you to make sure your money, time, and energy are invested in the right place.

Of course, money isn't the only way to give back. You can make a difference by giving your time, a helping hand, or a smile, or simply by lending an ear and listening to someone in need.

Inspo-action

Take a moment now to think about how you would like to give back this week. Again, remember, it doesn't have to be money. Think creatively—you are limited only by your imagination. So get your creative juices flowing! Jot down three ideas of how you can give back this week, then take action.

_____

_____

_____

Redefining Success on Your Terms

In the Western world, everyone seems to be chasing "success." According to the Oxford Dictionary, the definition of *success* is "the accomplishment of an aim or purpose" or "the attainment of fame, wealth, or social status."

For me, if I can put my head on my pillow at night and know that I have chosen love over fear, gently closed the door on my Mean Girl, done work that inspires me, made someone smile, hugged and kissed my little man, moved my body lovingly, been present, nourished my temple, spent time in nature, felt the sun on my skin, sat in stillness, taken time out for myself, and connected with my darling husband, then holy smokes, girlfriend, I have had a successful day.

Inspo-action

Life is full of missed opportunities, and it's very easy to read this book and not take action. Don't let that be you! Write down what your definition of success is. As with your beliefs around money, forget what the dictionary says or what people around you say—what is your definition of success?

_____

_____

_____

You can even get your whole family to do this exercise. Again, it all comes back to alignment—if you are super-duper clear on your definition of success, you'll be able to weed out anything (or anyone) that is not aligned to your higher truth.

Remember, being wildly wealthy, fabulously healthy, and bursting with love is not a giant leap. It's an inch-by-inch journey. And just like a tree is always either growing or dying, as long as you are constantly taking action and moving forward, you are growing and evolving. It's when we are standing still or going backward that we are dying.

WHAT ABOUT FINANCIAL SUCCESS?

The same principles apply for financial success. What do you believe in? What is your definition of financial success?

For some people it means owning a portfolio of properties, a fancy car, and some serious bling. Others see it as living without debt or being able to put a deposit on their first home or buy a plane ticket overseas. Whatever you believe is perfect! But make sure that your beliefs ring true for you and they aren't someone else's.

Personally, if I have enough money to do what I love each day, to feed my family nourishing food and clean water, to have a roof over my head, to travel, and to contribute to the world, then I am doing just fine.

Inspo-action

What is your definition of financial success? Whatever it is, don't let your Mean Girl creep in and take over. Stay connected to your heart and write whatever comes to you.

_____

_____

_____

From now on, it's your job to catch your Mean Girl when you aren't sticking to your definition of success and gently close the door on her. Reprogramming your thoughts and mastering your Mean Girl will take practice, but it's oh so worth it.

Playing *Big* and Stepping Up

Do you want to experience abundance in all areas of your life? Let me hear a *hell yeah!* Great! Now, I am not just talking about financial abundance here. I am talking about abundance in all areas of your life—your health and love too.

You already know how important your worthy-o-meter is for attracting good stuff to your life (in case you've forgotten, it needs to be cranked to the max!).

But to really manifest true abundance in your life, you've got to focus on two things: the energy you are vibrating at, and being open to the gifts and opportunities the Universe is sending you.

It's a universal law that what you put out you get back in return. If you want to have more, you must first become and give more.

Let go of your limiting Mean Girl beliefs that abundance isn't possible for you. We are all connected—all part of the same oneness—which means we are all able to experience abundance if we so wish. You must first decide that abundance is what you truly desire, then let go of your Mean Girl, dial up your worthy-o-meter, get out of your own way, stay open, and let it flow. Start there, my love. Go on, it's time to play big.

When my client Ella decided she wanted to let go of her limiting mind-set and switch to a more abundant belief system, she couldn't believe how quickly things started to flow for her. She was living in an uncomfortable share house and really wanted to move out on her own. At first she didn't feel worthy, but after a few sessions together we reprogrammed her beliefs and I taught her how to master her Mean Girl. Then the most amazing opportunity presented itself to her. A friend of a friend had to leave the country unexpectedly and needed someone to look after her cat in her beautiful studio apartment, and she didn't have time to list it on Airbnb. And because everything was so rushed, she offered the place to Ella rent free until she decided whether she was going to stay overseas or come back. See what happens when you master your Mean Girl? You open yourself up to opportunities you might not have seen if she was running the show.

Years ago, my then partner Tom and I were shopping at the farmers' market, chatting about how much we wanted to go away for his thirtieth birthday. We homed straight in on our ideal destination—a particular hotel that we loved in beautiful Byron Bay, which we knew would be perfect. We checked how much it was going to cost and decided to park the idea for the moment. But the seed had been planted. On the drive home we got a text message from his best friend reading, *Check your e-mail!* Not thinking anything of it, I unpacked our shopping while he jumped on his computer. Next thing I knew he was standing next to me with his laptop in his hands showing me the screen. It read, *Happy 30th birthday, mate! Enjoy your week-long deluxe spa pack with Melissa at Byron Bay,* and this was accompanied by a voucher for the *exact* hotel we'd been discussing earlier. Our jaws dropped.

Be open to abundance showing up in different forms. It doesn't have to show up only in the way of money. For Ella it showed up as a few months of rent-free accommodation, and for Tom it showed up in the form of a gift. Stay open and don't be married to the idea of it flowing to you solely in the form money.

Spirituality in the Twenty-first Century

I often hear women say, "I need to be more spiritual," or "That wasn't very spiritual of me"; or a really common one is "I want to meet a spiritual guy." But what does that actually mean?

All religion is a form of spirituality, the purpose being to bring you closer to God, the One, the Divine, Jesus, Love, the Source, Buddha . . . whatever you resonate with. But religion aside, let's talk spirituality.

First of all, being spiritual doesn't mean you have to wear white robes and move to the Himalayas. Spirituality is a state of being. It's an intuitive, deep-down knowingness that we are connected to all things everywhere. Spirituality says that even though you may think you are limited and small, you are not. You're greater and more powerful than you have ever imagined. You are magnificent and an almighty light exists within you, just as it lives within everyone and everything. There is no separation: just oneness. This means you are not limited by things like your race, sex, family, job title, marital status, bank balance, or your roles in life. Spirituality goes beyond that and says there is *so much more.* Spirituality focuses on the "inside" of life.

French philosopher Pierre Teilhard de Chardin is often credited with saying, "We are spiritual beings having a human experience," and I believe this to be true. "Experience" being the operative word. So what do you want to experience in this lifetime? None of us know how long we are here for, so why not start experiencing what your heart desires . . . today? Does your Mean Girl tell you that's not possible? Does she say you don't deserve that kind of abundance? Does she whisper that there are still so many things you need to do before you can be happy and content? That's a load of BS, so let's drop it right now and focus on the truth: we don't know how long we are here for, so we may as well make the most of it and live life to the fullest—right this very moment.

The weight of this potent truth really hit home for me when my bestie Jess passed on. And although it was heart-wrenchingly painful, one of the biggest lessons I got from that experience was how precious each and every single moment really is. All the things I was worrying about no longer seemed to matter with this type of life-changing perspective jolt.

I was always deeply inspired by how much Jess really lived each and every single moment to the absolute fullest. Despite living with cancer, she thrived—she never complained, never lost herself in a pity party, never stopped seeking joy, and always had the most beautiful smile plastered over her face. You see so many people these days just going through the motions. Not many are truly living. But she did and, boy, was it inspiring to watch.

So let me ask you this—do you feel like each day is Groundhog

Day? Are you just going through the motions of the "daily grind," or are you an active participant in life, seriously living each and every moment like it's your last?

Inspo-action

Let's make a commitment right now. Let's sign the sacred contract to live each and every moment to its fullest.

LIVE-IN-THE-MOMENT CONTRACT

I, _____, promise to live each and every single moment to its fullest. I will show up present, open, and wholeheartedly as my true and beautiful self.

This I promise!

Love, _____

Head to my website to download your free live-in-the-moment contract today.

The Material World versus the Spiritual World

To approach life materially is to rely chiefly on the empirical evidence provided by the five senses—what we can see, hear, taste, touch, or smell. Someone who is materialistic will constantly try to fix, change, and improve his or her outside world instead of looking within. The problem with this way of living is that the way you think and feel is dependent on your external world. Your measure of happiness, success, and joy is limited by the physical realm.

The spiritual world does not depend on the exterior. It goes beyond our five human senses—beyond the physical—and instead delves into the realm of intuition, energy, and love. Spirituality says that what you seek externally you already possess, meaning there's no need to search outside yourself—everything you need is already within you.

So are you living a material life or a spiritual life?

It's safe to say that the old me was definitely living a material life, but I am now so much more fulfilled living a spirit-driven life.

What Does a Spiritual Gal Look Like?

- Someone who is spiritual chooses love over fear in every moment.
- Her heart is her compass.
- She treats herself and all beings with the utmost love, care, and respect and knows that everything is interconnected.
- She truly knows deep down how magnificent she is.
- She nourishes the temple she's been given to house her soul.
- She lives a purposeful and passion-fueled life.
- She knows her mission and her *why* in life.
- She meets everyone with love.
- She is authentic and honest.
- She shares her unique gifts with the world.
- She is of service.

- She lets her uniqueness shine through.

- She has a soft heart.

- She doesn't compare.

- She knows that everything passes; that nothing is stagnant; and that our nature is to die, to birth, and to shed the old.

- She possesses a calm and grounded presence.

- She is present.

- She trusts in the flow of life and knows that everything is unfolding exactly the way it's meant to.

- She cherishes every moment and knows that life is a sacred gift from the divine source.

Being a Spiritual Gal in This Material World

I believe you can still be a spiritual girl in this material world. You *can* marry the two.

When I first started on my path to wellness, I didn't put anything toxic on or in my body; I swapped designer dresses for harem pants, cocktails for coconuts, TV for study, and partying for sipping herbal tea in the sunshine. I also started practicing yoga at five a.m., took up chanting and chakra dance, turned vegan, went to raw cacao parties, meditated three times a day, studied different philosophies, consulted powerful healers, visited shamans, rarely washed my hair, and even stopped shaving my armpits.

I needed to experience this complete polar opposite in order to have the space to find equilibrium, which is where I am at today. A spiritual girl in this material world.

Today, my happiness does not depend on material objects. *My happiness comes from within.* I now choose to live a very simple and minimal life. That doesn't mean I don't like nice clothes: I absolutely do. However, they do not complete or define me, and if I don't have them, it doesn't alter how I feel within or who I am. Before I hit rock bottom, I would have been devastated if I missed out on the latest pair of fashionable leather pants and would have searched high and low online to get my hands on a pair. Now, as I sit here and write this book, I am wearing a pair of old tracksuit pants, a gym jumper, my worn-out Ugg boots, zero makeup, and my hair in a messy bun. And I am content.

I believe we are here to evolve our human consciousness. God, the Universe, the One, Love (whatever you believe in) has given us the ultimate playground, and we are here on earth to relish in it. This includes appreciating beautiful sunsets, flowers, mountains, rain forests, oceans, the stars, and all the beauty Mother Nature has to offer. And it also includes enjoying the heck out of the latest pair of high heels, if you so wish. There is no shame if you are coming from love.

Don't let your Mean Girl fool you here—if those shoes are true for you, you'll know it, and everything about buying and wearing them will *feel* good deep in your core. If they're not aligned with your truth, you'll *feel* that too—whether it's a contracting feeling when you click "Add to Cart," a squirming in your stomach when you exit the shop, or a tiny twinge of guilt whenever you put them on. Listen to that. Remember, there is always a consequence when you choose fear instead of love.

Inspo-action

Find out if the way you are spending money is true for you or not. The next time you go to make a purchase, close your eyes and tune in to your body. Are you contracting or expanding? If you are contracting, then it's not true for you. If you are expanding, then it's safe to say it is.

Think of a recent time when you have purchased something and it made you feel expansive. Maybe it was when you bought a bunch of flowers, a warm winter woolly cardigan, or fresh produce from your farmers' market.

_____

_____

_____

Now think of a time when you purchased something and it made you contract. You felt sick in your belly, sweaty palms, and guilt galore. Maybe it was over those new shoes or that bottle of wine you didn't really need.

_____

_____

_____

Take note of how you feel when you exchange money: tune in and always do what's true for you and aligned to your core values.

HONORING YOURSELF AND MAKING THE EFFORT

It's also important to note that there's no shame in honoring yourself and taking pride in your appearance. Not only does looking after yourself and making the effort make you *feel* good from deep within, but it's a beautiful act of self-love and a simple way of saying, "I love, honor, and respect myself."

A little example: occasionally, if I'm not tuning in to my truth and am feeling lazy, I'll head straight from my morning yoga session to my office to start my workday—sweaty workout gear and all. All morning, I'll feel icky, uninspired, and flat. The feeling lifts only when I finally tune in to my truth and take a shower, brush my hair, and put on some jeans and a nice top. I instantly feel *so* much better, and when I sit back down at my desk, inspiration inevitably starts to flow again. So take the time to make a little extra effort in the morning, even if you work at home or for yourself. It's a form of self-love and will make a massive difference to the energy you take into your day.

Being Wildly Wealthy Recap

- Remember, money is just energy.
- When you spend your money, always ask yourself, "Is this aligned to me and my core values?"
- Stay true to your definition of success.
- Choose to have an abundance mind-set.
- Spirituality is a state of being.

SEVEN

divine relationships

The purpose of relationship is not to have another
who might complete you; but to have another with
whom you might share your completeness.

NEALE DONALD WALSCH, *Conversations with God*

Before we dive into the world of relationships, I want to ask you a question: who are the five most prominent people in your life? Maybe it's your partner, your mum, your bestie, your boss, or the girl who sits next to you at work. (For all the mamas out there, this doesn't include your children—right now I am referring to the adult relationships in your life.) Whoever it is, write down your top five, and then take a long, hard look at your answers.

_____

_____

These top five relationships are a direct reflection of you.

You see, we are a product of the people we surround ourselves with. Which means that whoever you're hanging out with the most says a lot about who you are and who you are becoming.

With that in mind, when you look at your list, is your immediate reaction, "Oh crap!"? Or did you think, *"Hell yeah*, that's awesome—these people are *amazing*; I am so inspired by them and so grateful to have them in my life!" If your answer was more like the first, it might be time for a relationship reassessment.

When I look back at the relationships I had before I turned my life around, I can see they were definitely a reflection of my internal state. I don't regret anything in life—those relationships were perfect for where I was at in my journey, and I learned so many beautiful lessons along the way—but they were certainly not serving my higher good and I wasn't serving theirs.

Once you realize the importance of the relationships in your life, you can then make a choice. You can continue to give your time, energy, and space to those relationships, or you can not. This doesn't mean you have to go and break up with your bestie via text right now. It's simply an opportunity to look closely at the prominent people and connections in your life and ask yourself some serious questions: Do your relationships inspire you and allow you to be the fullest version of your authentic self? Or are they causing you to shrink and become a modified version of yourself? The answers will tell you a lot.

Sometimes the people sucking your energy might be family members or bosses, and removing yourself from the situation isn't feasible, so a good question to ask is, "What changes do *I* need to make within or to that relationship to make it more inspiring and healthy for me?" This might mean steering conversations away from the stale, familiar gossip sessions, or instead of meeting for cocktails meet for a coconut.

Inspo-action

Start to think about some small tweaks you could make to your relationships to make them more inspiring. Jot down your ideas.

_____

_____

_____

_____

Relationships allow us the opportunity to be the fullest versions of ourselves. They allow us to expand into higher consciousness.

If a relationship doesn't inspire the bejesus out of you, then why would you continue to entertain it and give it your energy? Sometimes our Mean Girl tells us that we "should" because it's the "right" thing to do, but what is your truth saying? Maybe your truth is to no longer sit and listen to one person or another bitch about how crappy his life is, how they always have no money, and how much her partner annoys her because he never does anything around the house. **Your time, energy, and space are very precious, so be careful who you give them to.** And with those people you *do* choose to give your energy to, give like your life depends on it—give love with your whole heart and don't hold back an inch. Because remember, what you put out you get back. And if you want more love in your life you must first give more love to yourself and to all things.

Whatever you decide, remember that every relationship in your life serves a divine purpose. Those people are there to enrich your heart, teach you something, and provide a sacred opportunity for divine growth. And that's the purpose you serve for them too!

Whatever relationships you have attracted in your life at this moment are precisely the ones you need in your life at this moment. There is a hidden meaning behind all events, and this hidden meaning is serving your own evolution.

DEEPAK CHOPRA

Your relationships are your biggest spiritual assignments. ***As humans, we are hardwired for connection and thrive on love and intimacy.*** So don't deny yourself, but do choose wisely. Your choices affect your actions and your actions affect your life, both today and in the future.

It's also important to mention you aren't going to connect with everyone. That's the beautiful thing about polarity: there is no need to be falsely loving just to be nice. If you meet someone you don't connect with, ask yourself why. What is it about her or him that doesn't align? Take a look in the mirror. Does something about that person remind you of you? What is triggering you? There will be some nuggets of wisdom in there if you take some time to dig for them.

Recently my friend Vanessa and I were having a chat on the phone when she told me she thinks Michelle (a mutual friend) is in-authentic. Before we went any further I asked where she is being in-authentic in her own life. The question took her by surprise, but because she was open she stopped to think about it. I could hear her crying as she realized she was being inauthentic in her relationship. If she hadn't stopped to look in the mirror, it's quite possible she would have missed that opportunity to get honest with herself.

Remember, every relationship is a reflection of you. Take the time to stop and look in the mirror before you throw around the judgments.

Whose Stuff Is It Anyway?

A few years back, I accidentally cut someone off in the car park at my local shopping center. I knew I hadn't been paying enough attention and the incident was my fault. I quickly mouthed, "I'm sorry," and gave a sincere wave to the man in the car behind me. The man got out of his car, came up to my window, and started abusing me. Fists were being waved, spittle was flying, and vulgar language was hurled in my direction. I was hurt and extremely shocked—it had seemed like a minor incident, and I had immediately apologized. His reaction seemed crazily disproportionate.

Shaken, I drove around the corner, pulled into a parking spot, and promptly burst into tears. I knew I needed to be more present while driving—I had been distracted by my phone ringing and someone could have been hurt—so I was grateful for the potent reminder. But I was also really taken aback by the man's reaction. *How could he be so mean? I didn't do it on purpose: it was an accident!* I thought.

It was a powerful way to learn an important lesson about relationships: in all our human interactions, **everyone is dealing with** *their own stuff.* <u>Every single person has his or her own pains, fears, frustrations, and concerns.</u> In that moment in the car park, the other man's reaction had been about *his* stuff. Maybe he had just been fired or his cat had died or he'd found out his grandma was in the hospital—really, the reason was none of my business. He'd simply been angry and frustrated and I just happened to be the person on the receiving end, which in turn was perfect for me because it was the slap in the face I needed.

Realizing this truth helped me get perspective, and it made me conscious of the fact that the only thing I could control in the whole situation was my own reaction. In fact, when you understand that people will always try to project their own stuff onto you, it's quite liberating. It helps you let go. It means you can stop taking things personally and will save you years of Mean Girl battles in your mind.

You see, everyone is always seeking unity. Some people may want to bring you down to their level, and others may want to raise you up. Either way your job is to stand in *your* truth and remember that *everyone is always seeking unity.*

Realizing this is a great opportunity for growth. If someone projects their stuff onto you and you remain calm and neutral, then you can happily walk away knowing that it was *their* emotional baggage and had nothing to do with you. However, if someone projects their stuff and it triggers something within you—say, anger, frustration, or sadness—then, my friend, there is an opportunity for your own personal evolution right there. You can either grasp that opportunity with both hands or you can project your own stuff right back at them and totally miss the nugget of wisdom buried underneath. The choice is yours. The key is to be super conscious and present so you can see what's *really* going on. If you let your Mean Girl take over, you'll squander a beautiful opportunity for growth.

Mirror, Mirror on the Wall

Sometimes we're the ones projecting our stuff onto others. I remember an incident years ago, in London, when I'd gone to Starbucks with my friend Megan. We were catching up with a new friend, Mia. After we'd had our gossip and finished our grande caramel lattes and banana bread lathered in margarine, we said good-bye to her and began walking home. Megan commented on how sweet, funny, and bubbly she thought Mia was. I, on the other hand, had thought she was stuck-up and fake.

Isn't it funny how two people can have very different opinions of the same experience and the same person? Of course, there was a lesson to be learned from my bitching. *When we judge others, we are simply judging ourselves. What we see in others is some truth about ourselves.*

In that moment at the Starbucks, what I saw in Mia was what I feared within myself. She triggered my own stuff. I was simply looking in the mirror at my own reflection. There was an element of stuck-up-ness and inauthenticity radiating out of me and that was being bounced back at me through Mia. Mia was my mirror.

Now, whenever I feel myself go to judge someone, I take a look in the mirror and remind myself that it has nothing to do with the other person and everything to do with me. Your Mean Girl won't want you to look at yourself honestly like that, but do it anyway. Free yourself today.

Understanding this mirror concept will save you years of heartache and will fast-track your journey to master your Mean Girl.

Expectation Overload

We've already discussed how having expectations of yourself and others can fuel your Mean Girl's fire and set you up for a painful overload. Our Mean Girl often attaches expectations to the people nearest and dearest to us—*she's my best friend so she should treat me a certain way; she's my sister so she should do this for me.* Not only is this denying your truth—and the truth of those around you—but it's incredibly exhausting and will lead you quickly down the path to unhappiness. We need to quit *should*-ing all over the place, let go of our expectations, and accept the truth of the present moment and of the people around us. Wouldn't you rather someone did something for you because he wanted to with all his heart, not because he felt he should?

Growing up in a strict Italian-Catholic family, I watched my mother, father, and everyone around me do things for everyone else because they *"should."* This became deeply ingrained in me, and from a young age I constantly people pleased, because that was what I saw everyone else doing. I also developed the belief that you *"should"* do things to make other people happy and that it didn't matter if you had to sacrifice your own truth and happiness in the process. It wasn't until I hit rock bottom that I realized I needed to put my own health and happiness first, and that I was no good to anyone else if I wasn't at my best.

Every time we people please, we are saying yes to someone else and no to ourselves. In that moment, we are well and truly diminishing our light. Nothing good comes out of people pleasing, just that old "expectation overload"—a yucky feeling deep in your gut and a sour taste in your mouth.

Don't think I am saying you shouldn't do things for other people. I am constantly doing nice things for my family, friends, and team; however, it's not because I feel like I "should," but simply because I love to. There's a definite difference. One is motivated by fear and the other by love. When you are coming from love, the energy is different—not only will *you* feel it, but so will the person on the receiving end.

To avoid giving yourself an icky expectation overload, drop the labels and expectations you place on yourself, your family, and your friends and just show up as your beautiful self. And stop *should*-ing all over the place.

Comparisonitis

I used to suffer from a serious case of comparisonitis. I lived in a constant state of not feeling good enough. I compared everything about me to others—how I looked, the work I did, how much money I made, how many clients I had, the clothes I wore, how much I weighed, the car I drove, how happy I was . . . *everything*! I did it because I was insecure within myself, and my Mean Girl was having a field day. It was one of my most sensitive pain points, and she pushed on it whenever she could.

Soul Share

Comparison keeps you stuck in Fear Town.
It will rob you of happiness and pure joy.

When you compare yourself, you are coming from fear (your Mean Girl), which is the opposite of your truth (love). Your Mean Girl uses comparison to keep you in a state of suffering and out of your heart. That's her job and the way she survives. Remember, **your Mean Girl _cannot_ survive in a state of love.** So she will do whatever it takes (like point out your friends' successes on Facebook, the beautiful skin of some celebrity on Instagram, and even the great shoes on a girl walking down the street) to keep love at bay and guarantee her power over you. It's just another sneaky Mean Girl trick!

Comparison keeps you small and creates a scarcity mind-set.

When I was in comparison mode, nothing flowed in my life. I would compare how many clients I had with other coaches, then couldn't work out why I struggled to find more. I would compare my bank balance with other people's, then couldn't work out why I never experienced abundance. I compared my relationship with other relationships, then was flabbergasted when it flopped. I compared how I looked with everyone around me, then wondered why I could never change my weight or get my hair just the way I wanted it.

As soon as I saw what was really going on, I remembered that I had a choice: as with everything in life, I could choose to come from love or stay in fear. Thankfully, I chose the first option, and I want to encourage you to do the same.

Remember, it's just a choice—*your* choice.

I am still human and my Mean Girl does still try to compare me to others; however, it is nothing like it used to be. I am excited to say that, now that I've gotten over my full-blown comparisonitis and live from a place of love, everything flows so much more freely—my work, my relationships, my health, and my finances. I am content in my own skin and, best of all, it's effortless.

My friendships have also changed. Back then, it was like a competition—who could be the thinnest, happiest, and most success-ful. Now, though, instead of gossiping about who's skinnier, who landed the biggest gig, or who kissed the hottest guy on Saturday night, we talk about positive stuff and genuinely celebrate one an-other's wins . . . Oh, how things have changed!

Maybe the biggest difference of all is that we are completely au-thentic with one another—there are no masks, cover-ups, or facades. Gone are those days. Now we can just be ourselves. How refreshing!

Take a moment to reflect on the relationships in your life: are they based on comparison? Gently remind yourself to slide back into your heart (it's so much warmer in there). Be grateful for these relationships, choose to come from love, let your Mean Girl take a backseat, and instead of comparing yourself to those people, praise them for their greatness, celebrate their wins, and genuinely be happy for them.

How to Treat a Soul Sister 101

Your soul sisters are the friends who really *get* you, deep down. There's no pretending, no hiding, no comparing, and no competition—just pure, genuine love and joy. They're the ones you're not afraid to share your truth with, they're always there when you need them, and they never try to dim your light.

My soul sisters are kicking major goals right now—becoming authors, touring, overcoming health issues, being asked to speak at TED, launching game-changing online programs, busting through limiting beliefs, getting married, starting a family, and choosing love over fear. The old me would have felt seriously threatened by their success. But now I feel incredibly inspired by them. In fact, I am their biggest cheerleader and number one fan.

In order to have authentic, soul-deep friendships, you have to stop comparing and let go of the fear-based thinking. Your Mean Girl will still pipe up, but the more you can catch her in the act, the easier it gets.

If you want to build and nurture authentic relationships with your soul sisters, follow these guidelines:

- When something big happens in her life, show genuine happiness for her. Celebrate her wins, loudly and proudly. Write her a card, drop off some flowers from your garden, or take her for a green juice.
- Always be her biggest cheerleader and support her unconditionally.
- Inspire her to be the best version of herself.

℗ Love her unconditionally.

℗ Let go of your expectations.

℗ Share how you're feeling.

℗ Listen—and I mean *really* listen—to what she is saying, without interrupting.

℗ Don't give your opinion until it has been asked for.

℗ Put down your phone when she is sharing with you and be one hundred percent present.

℗ Send her love, always.

℗ Feel inspired by her greatness.

℗ Don't ever judge her.

℗ Let your soul sister cry when she needs to, and never, ever stop her. Just hold space for her to get it all out. That's what real friends are for.

Inspo-action

It's super important that we nurture our goddess relationships. So take a moment now to write down all the soul sisters in your life. Next to each name, write one thing you love about that person.

_____

_____

_____

_____

_____

_____

_____

_____

_____

_____

Your job now is to let them know it. You could send them a text message, write them a letter, or pick up the phone. However you want to roll is fine; just let them know how freaking awesome they are and how much you value them. Even a _thinking of you_ or _sending you love_ text is perfect.

Frenemies, Energy Vampires, and Drawing Boundaries

It's awesome to have meaningful relationships with your soul sisters and other loved friends. But we can also find ourselves in relationships with people who are actually dragging us down and making us feel like crap. You know the type of people I mean—maybe it's the "friend" who always gives you backhanded compliments that truly sting, or the girl you've known since high school who calls only when she needs something (and is never around when you've got your own stuff going on), or maybe it's a whole gang of peeps you used to hang out with whose values no longer align with your own . . .

Whatever type of "friend" it is that's pulling you down, there are some things you can do to protect yourself and ensure that your energy isn't being compromised.

1. _Recognize that all relationships serve a divine purpose._
   Yep, even that "friend" who _really_ knows how to push your

buttons. There is a lesson you need to learn from this person, and the sooner you figure it out, the sooner you can both move on and let the experience go.

2. *Know that you do not have to put up with being treated badly.*

It doesn't matter whether you've known someone since you were both toddlers, or if you feel bad for them because they've got no other friends (which is a judgment, by the way), or any other reason that you might be telling yourself. The simple truth is this: you deserve to be treated with kindness and respect by the people around you, and anyone who is not living up to this standard is not worth your time and energy.

3. *Choose to prioritize your own needs and energy state.*

When it comes to frenemies and energy vampires, many of us find it difficult to stand our ground and assert our boundaries . . . which is why you can find yourself hanging out with them (or helping them move house, or pet-sitting their pooch even though you're allergic to dogs) time and time again. In these situations, it's important that you recognize that the only person who's going to stand up for your needs is *you*. You have the power to choose who you spend your time with, and you need to be the one prioritizing your own needs.

4. *Lovingly but firmly assert your boundaries.*

If you don't want to hang out with someone, don't! When you are asked, kindly but firmly state your truth. If your knee-jerk reaction is to always say yes, try to give yourself a little breathing space to help gather your thoughts: *Thank you so much for thinking of me; let me check my calendar and get back to you.*

5. *Stand by your no.*

If you've asserted your boundaries, stand by them. Remember: we teach other people how to treat us. If you don't respect your own boundaries, or if you'll bend them at the first sign of tension, why would anyone else bother to respect your boundaries? In the wise words of Brené Brown, "choose discomfort over resentment." Meaning, it's better to make a choice that is aligned with your truth—even when it's really tough—than to fall into the murky energy of resentment and ill will. So even though saying no can be hard, in these types of situations, it's really, truly worth it.

I have a rule that if something is not an absolute *hell yeah*, then it's a no. So if I am hemming and hawing about whether I should go to an event or speak at a conference, or stymied over which couch to buy, then it's a no.

6. *If all else fails, lovingly let them go.*

If you've tried your best to assert your boundaries and include someone in your life in a way that serves both of you, yet they haven't given an inch . . . it's time to focus your energy elsewhere. It may sound harsh, but the reality is that you can *never* control how someone else acts, and putting up with being treated poorly is not doing *either* of you any favors. Kindly, gently detach them from your energy field. Some people like to physically tell the other person that they need some space; others prefer a slow, gentle fade-out. Whichever way feels more genuine and kind to you, make sure that you are sending the other person unconditional love the whole time and honoring your truth. That way, your own energy will remain clear and light, and you can both continue your soul journeys unencumbered by negativity.

Inspo-action

Who do you need to say a loving no to in your life? Make a list of the people and situations in your life that are draining your energy. For each one, what is the boundary you need to assert? What are you no longer willing to do or put up with?

_____

_____

_____

_____

_____

Write out an affirmation that can help you assert these boundaries with love and kindness. It could be something like this: *"I am a strong, powerful woman and I lovingly stand in my truth"*; or you can craft your own. Stick your affirmation up around the house where you'll be reminded of it every day.

The Most Important Relationship of All

While we're busy discussing our relationships with others, and before we delve into the divine topic of soul mates and romantic love, it's an excellent time to revisit the one relationship that underpins everything else in your life—you guessed it, the one with yourself.

There's no point in addressing your relationships with the people around you if you're not practicing what you preach with yourself. You still must be flexing that self-love muscle, cranking up your worthy-o-meter, and believing in yourself. No amount of romantic wizardry or friendship fine-tuning will make up for a lousy relationship with yourself; you've got to seriously commit to treating yourself with nothing but straight-up love.

Inspo-action

Let's get serious! It's time to commit to loving yourself.

SELF-LOVE CONTRACT

I, _____, commit to loving you unconditionally and wholeheartedly.

- I will honor and respect you.
- I will stay true to you always.
- I will treat you with the utmost love and care.
- I will listen to my heart and not my head.
- I will choose love over fear in every moment.

> I will breathe deeply.
>
> I will cherish each moment.
>
> I will give freely.
>
> I will stay open and look at the world through soft eyes.
>
> I will make self-care my number one priority always.
>
> Thank you for choosing me to house your beautiful spirit for this lifetime.
>
> I love you.
>
> Signed _____
>
> Date _____

You can head on over to my website and grab your free self-love contract. Print it out, sign it, and stick it somewhere so you can see it daily and remind yourself of the pledge you made to your beautiful self.

Calling In Your Soul Mate

It's not until you have cultivated a loving relationship with yourself that you will be able to call in your soul mate. Until then, you'll just experience romantic relationships that fill a void but aren't quite right. You will be settling and denying yourself and things will always feel a little off.

I had to create space in my life before I was ready to meet my soul mate. At twenty-eight years old, I married the man of my dreams—my soul mate and lover for life. But to get there, I had to karate-chop my limiting beliefs, master my Mean Girl, let go of the past, heal my heart, get healthy, love myself, and learn some pretty big life lessons. I'm definitely not saying that everyone has to experience what I experienced before they find their soul mate, but you do have to be at a place within yourself where you are bursting with love before your soul mate can enter the picture.

Before I met my husband, I dated a lovely guy. Our relationship was great—we laughed, had similar interests, and deeply cared about each other. But I always knew deep down that he wasn't "the one." Actually I knew that deep down with all my past relationships. But during those years I didn't even know if "the one" existed—I didn't believe in marriage, finding "the one," or soul mates; I didn't want to have kids; and I was seriously confused about our future together.

We started our relationship when I was at a very low point in my life—around the time of the big breakdown that changed everything. He came into my life and filled a massive void within me, and I did the same for him. Our relationship served a beautiful purpose for both of our evolutions. We are still friends today, because we can see that our time together was part of each of our journeys. I will be forever grateful for him and our experience.

It took a lot of balls to leave that relationship. After all, on the surface, nothing was wrong. We didn't hate each other, we never fought, but it just didn't *feel* right. It was safe and secure, and the thought of leaving scared the crap out of me. Ending it would mean dramatic change—we shared a house, furniture, friends . . . How was I going to just walk away from all of that?

However, the fear wasn't enough reason to stay. When we did eventually part ways, I instantly felt a weight lift off my shoulders. I knew it was the right decision, but that certainly didn't mean it was easy.

The following months were really tough. I went deep inside and practiced some serious self-love. I spent many days alone—journaling, meditating, crying, praying, peeling back the layers, letting go, unlearning old habits, battling with my Mean Girl—until the fog slowly began to lift. All the inner work I had been doing was starting to pay off. The tears stopped flowing, the heaviness in my chest subsided, my Mean Girl quieted down, and my worthy-o-meter was dialed right up.

For the first time in my life, I started to feel like *me*—the real me, the true me. There was finally space in my life.

Months went by, and I continued to practice truly loving myself. I enjoyed my own company and was having a ball getting to spend so much quality time alone doing things I loved.

Then one day, out of the blue, I got a text from Nick: *Do you want to do yoga and meditation tomorrow morning with me on the beach?*

My heart skipped a beat, and it was a whole-body *yes*.

We had known each other for about three years before we got together, but we had both been in long-term relationships. We had many mutual friends and had actually sat across from each other at dinner once (although we spoke very few words). For years we would bump into each other—and hardly speak. If our life was a cartoon, it was like there was a cloud over him—I can't even really remember him being there. I believe that's because we weren't ready to *really* meet yet. The Universe had a divine plan for us, and the time wasn't yet right. We had too much inner work and soul searching still to do.

When we finally got together, we were both at a place in our lives where we were very content. Neither of us felt like we "needed" another person; we had all the love we required within ourselves. We had both learned not to place expectations on another person or on a relationship.

When two people who are overflowing with love decide to join, magic is sure to follow.

During our first couple of dates, we sat—eyes locked and hearts beating—and talked for hours. We were open, authentic, vulnerable, and raw. There was no censoring and no expectations on each other, because we had nothing to lose—I was whole within myself and so was he.

Guess what happens when two people are aligned and whole within themselves? Unity! Within days, we fell madly, deeply, passionately, wholeheartedly in love. There was no fear and no doubt. See what happens when you get out of the way and leave your baggage at the door? A few dates in, I texted my bestie: *He's the one.*

Two weeks later there he was, on one knee with an extremely rare sapphire (the stone of destiny), asking me to marry him. Six months later we were married, and I still pinch myself every single morning I open my eyes and see his beautiful face right there. I didn't think it was possible to fall in love with someone more and more each day but now I know it's true.

MEAN GIRL MOMENT

I've been asked many times via social media or e-mail to share the story of our love, but I always held off. I wasn't sure why until I sat and wrote this section of my book, and it finally became clear to me. As I typed the words, my Mean Girl reared her head: *Don't brag, Melissa: no one cares about your love.* Boy, we humans are amazing at shrinking right when we should be celebrating, aren't we?

This relationship is beyond my wildest dreams. It's exactly what fairy tales are made of. Every day we experience a deeper, more passionate, more bountiful love for each other. He is my soul mate, my anchor, my one-and-only; and I am madly, passionately, and deeply in love with him. Why should I suppress that? Why should I play it down? I believe we need to celebrate love *more*. Love is our birthright, it's our lifeblood, and it's such a beautiful thing to share with the world.

Do you find yourself shrinking so that others don't feel uncomfortable? It's time to stop that and start to celebrate you, your wins, love, or whatever you like.

Inspo-action

Write down a time when you have dimmed your light in order not to make someone else feel insecure.

_____

_____

_____

_____

Now write down all the things you haven't yet celebrated but want to. Maybe it's hosting a dinner party and
cooking a slow-cooked lamb shoulder for the first time,
getting the kids in bed early, a big win at work, or finally
learning how to back up your phone. No matter how big
or small, I believe life is here to be celebrated—even the
smaller things.

_____

_____

_____

_____

Entering a divine relationship with your soul mate is like signing
a contract with love itself.

When there is unity, clarity, alignment, and consciousness in a
divine relationship, there is no place to hide. If you are not being the
fullest version of yourself, your partner immediately calls you on
it—he or she won't settle for anything less.

My darling won't let me get away with anything. If he can see
me skipping toward Fear Town holding hands with my Mean Girl,
he won't stand for it. He will, however, *inspire* me out of it. That is
his job and the promise we made to each other the day we got married, and although I sometimes want to kick and scream and throw
myself a pity party, I realize that it's all part of being in a divine
relationship.

To be honest, my entire view on what being in a relationship en-
tails has shifted since we got together. I now believe **we enter a**

partnership to inspire and support the other person to be the fullest expression of him- or herself. We enter a partnership to be of full service to *that* person's evolution, because by doing so, in turn, we are serving our own.

The Seven Laws of a Divine Relationship

For two people to experience a divine relationship, both people must first:

1. Have their worthy-o-meter cranked up high.
2. Be authentic.
3. Be living a life of purpose.
4. Be flexing their self-love muscle daily.
5. Understand that in order to serve themselves, they must be of service to their partner.
6. Be ready to take full responsibility for their own crap, their own limiting beliefs, and their own emotional baggage.
7. Use love as their compass and let their hearts lead the way.

Before my darling came along I never thought a divine relationship was possible. But it is! Marrying him was the easiest thing I have ever done. And the truth is, *all of us* can experience divine relationships.

Are you ready to live the seven laws of a divine relationship and call in your soul mate? Then do it, beautiful. Your time is now. Or, if you're already in a divine relationship, how can you take it to the next level?

Inspo-action

It's time to call in more beautiful, aligned relationships in your life. Close your eyes, open your heart, and say out loud, "I am ready for inspiring souls, aligned spirits, and divine relationships to enter my life. I hold the space for them to unfold."

Write down five women you admire and would like to connect with:

_____

_____

_____

_____

_____

Now take action. Reach out to these women this week. Start with a heartfelt e-mail or pick up the phone. Share with them why you love them or their work and how much you would love to take them out for a cuppa.

Divine Relationships Recap

- Relationships allow us the opportunity to be the fullest versions of ourselves.
- Your relationships are your biggest spiritual assignments.
- When we judge others, we are simply judging ourselves. What we see *in others is some truth about ourselves.*
- Every time we people please, we are saying yes to

someone else and no to our truth. In that moment we are dimming our light.

ↂ Comparison keeps you in Fear Town. It will rob you of happiness and pure joy.

ↂ Quit comparing.

ↂ Treat your soul sisters with love.

ↂ The most important relationship is the relationship with yourself. You must cultivate a loving relationship with your awesome self first.

ↂ Unity, clarity, alignment, and consciousness are prerequisites for divine relationships.

Living from Love Checklist

Now that you've finished part two of this book, you know that living from a place of love is essential for creating a life beyond your wildest dreams. The following affirmations represent the wisdom you've unlocked in this section and will encourage you to embed these principles in your daily life. I invite you to print them out from my website, put them somewhere prominent, and really set the intention of embodying them every day.

☐ I know that honoring my body is an act of self-love.

☐ I let passion pump my pulse.

☐ I see money as energy, and I am consciously creating a wildly wealthy life.

☐ I love myself first, and I am actively calling in divine relationships.

PART THREE

Bursting with Love

your gift to the world

Only the truth of who you are,
if realized, will set you free.

ECKHART TOLLE

The biggest gift you can give to the world is your authentic self. That truly is the most important job you have on this planet—to be the most authentic version of yourself. Like Eckhart Tolle says, when you realize this, you will be free. Yet it's something that so many of us struggle with all our lives.

I remember when I was in primary school that I wanted to be more like the popular girls. I wanted to look like them, act like them, and be interested in the same things as them. I even started copying the way the most popular girl walked and talked. She sat a particular way—with one leg crossed over the other—so I tried to emulate that too, perfecting my technique at home to get it just right. Clearly I was so desperate to be seen as "popular" and "cool" that I was even willing to change my whole self in the process.

Throughout my life, I have heard many people say *Just be your-self,* but I never really grasped the potency of that statement. I had to do a lot more learning (and unlearning) before I was ready to really embody me and my true essence. I first had to find out who the real me actually was.

Starting my own business was an important part of my authenticity "learning curve." For the first year or so after I began blogging, I slightly censored myself and presented a version of myself that I thought was "appealing." I didn't give away too much, out of fear of being rejected and not being accepted—I was so scared of what other people might think of me. As a result, business was pretty crappy that year. I had only a few clients, my blog wasn't getting a lot of visitors, and I averaged about two comments per post. It's fair to say things weren't flowing effortlessly. Then one day, I wrote a very deep and vulnerable post about my struggle with food and my relationship with my body and—*boom!* The amount of "likes" I got quadrupled. The number of unique visitors to my website tripled and the comments went ballistic. I was in total shock and it wasn't until I sat down and pondered what had happened that it occurred to me:

All I have to do is be me, share my truth, and speak from my heart.

As I sit here and write this book I'm nursing a serious vulnerability hangover. *Have I overshared? Have I revealed too much? What are they going to think of me?* My Mean Girl wants to prod those old sore spots. (See, I told you mine still pops up!) But as I pat her hand and pass her a cup of psychic tea, I realize she is still petrified of being judged, desperate to be liked, and craving acceptance from other people. My true self doesn't care: my true self wants to share my stories in order to inspire you into *your* brilliance. So right now in this moment I have one of two choices: I can close down my computer and not turn in my manuscript, or I can stare my Mean Girl in the face and say, *You will not win*. The choice is always mine.

Being vulnerable makes people lean in.

People have liked my Facebook page, signed up to my newsletter, and followed me on Twitter and Instagram because they *want* to hear from me—and all I have to do is be me. How liberating! No more trying to be something I'm not.

This principle has held true for the hundreds of women I've worked with as well. They would come to me struggling with their online business—often after spending thousands of dollars trying to get their website off the ground—but there was no "them" in what they were doing. I would always suggest that they add more of themselves to their website and products, whether through photos, in their copy, by adding personal stories, or just by writing more in their own "voice"—and *boom*. The same thing would happen. Almost instantly, they'd get more sales, sign-ups, likes, and followers. It happened every time. Why? Because humans are hardwired for connection. We want to feel like someone gets us. We don't want to land on a person's website and feel like she has a "perfect" life. People can't relate to that—they relate to *real* people and *real* life situations. This is why being your true self is so important and will trump even the slickest marketing campaign any day. Same goes for mothers' groups. I've had so many clients and friends call me in tears after the latest mothers' group catch-up because so-and-so says her baby sleeps all through the night and eats whatever she puts in front of her. Now, maybe that's true, but there's a chance it's not. Be truthful and authentic in each moment and just be you. It's your sacred birthright to be your authentic self. No one wants you to be anything but, so there's no need to portray this "perfect" life.

Never underestimate the potency and power of simply being yourself and having the courage to share it with the world.

Inspo-action

Write down everything about you that makes you unique, everything that makes you *you*. The silly jokes that only you find hilarious, your love and passion for animals, your mad hip-hop dancing skills—once you have made your list, read it back to yourself and really own it. Be proud of your quirkiness and know that your uniqueness is what makes you so perfectly *you*.

_____

_____

_____

_____

_____

_____

_____

_____

_____

Being authentic doesn't come easy to someone who has had years and years of conditioning, but it *is* your birthright. It might take a little work to figure out which of your beliefs are actually your own, and what living authentically really means to you, but once you've tuned in to your truth, the freedom you'll experience will fill your heart to the brim.

Living authentically *feels* really good, but there's an even more serious reason to embrace your truth: when we *don't* live truthfully, it's actually hurting us. You see, when we suppress our authenticity, it festers away inside us. It boils under our skin waiting to be expressed. Your true essence is a desire to live as your full, beautiful self, so don't deny it. Don't play small, dim your light, shrink down, or censor yourself. And don't be afraid of the brilliance that lies within you.

Are you playing small and shrinking so that others around you won't feel insecure? It's time to stop that right now and let out your beautiful true self—the world needs your shining, radiant essence.

Inspo-action

The dress rehearsal for life is over: *this is it!* It's time to stop shrinking and let out your true self.

AUTHENTICITY CONTRACT

I, _____, promise to be my authentic self.

> ✎ I promise to never dim my light.
>
> ✎ I promise to shine as bright as I can and never shrink in order to make other people comfortable.
>
> ✎ I promise to be my true, beautiful self and stand in my power always.
>
> This I promise.
>
> Signed _____
>
> Date _____

Jump on over to my website and grab your free printable authenticity contract. Once you've printed and signed it, use it as a daily reminder of your deep commitment to living your truth.

Coping with Criticism

When you reveal your authentic self, you expose yourself to ridicule and criticism. It can be really tough, especially if you're not used to it. But remember, everybody has an opinion and there's nothing you can do about that. But the sooner you stop caring what other people think of you, the sooner you will be set free.

The first time I got a nasty comment on my website, I cried. Actually, the first, second, and maybe even third time that someone posted something negative on my website, I got upset. *Why doesn't this person like me? I didn't do anything to them; all I am trying to do is help people,* I'd think. I'd spend hours worrying about it and try-ing to figure out what I should do differently next time so that they'd like me and my work. But you *cannot* please everyone. Haters are always gonna hate.

Eventually, I realized that my efforts to appease random strang-ers were not only pointless, they were also keeping me from being my true, radiant self. The truth is, *what other people think of you is none of your business.* Allowing myself to let go of that worry and angst was extremely liberating, and it freed up so much energy.

Now, after years of exposing my true self through my live events, products, website, books, and programs, and on social media, I've figured out that there are three different types of people who'll be attracted to you and the work you're putting out into the world:

1. Raving fans who love you
2. People who dislike you
3. People who don't care and are neutral

Your job isn't to preach to the people from categories two and three, it's to focus on the people in category one—the people you are already serving. *They* are your tribe. They are the people who want to hear from you. That is where you need to focus your energy and time, not trying to convert the others.

To this day I occasionally get people saying nasty things—heck, there will probably be people who say nasty things over this book—but my intention is not to let their words affect me anymore. In fact, I like to energetically send love and light in their direction. I figure that for someone to go to the effort of writing something nasty about another person, they must be in a pretty bad space themselves. So I send them love, wish them peace, and let it go.

I also believe that people shouldn't really criticize others unless they are in the arena themselves, putting themselves on the line. I am constantly digging deep, sharing from my heart, being raw, and nursing vulnerability hangovers—it's a very exposed place to be, but I wouldn't have it any other way. If someone who is *not* out there putting their heart on the line tries to criticize me—someone who doesn't truly understand what it's like and what it takes—then I don't even bother listening. Seriously. Unless the person knows what it's like to have skin in the game, his or her opinion is null and void in my eyes. If, on the other hand, my husband, one of my team, a customer, or a loyal tribe member gives me feedback I will listen with an open heart, digest their words, sit with it, and see what it means for me. There are usually some nuggets of wisdom in there, and their feedback matters to me.

Inspo-action

If you want to take things to the next level and *really* protect yourself from negativity, try my protection meditation so that no one can zap your energy. Head over to my website to get instant access to it.

When critics strike, go back to the mirror concept and know that if someone has an issue with you or your work, it has nothing to do with you and everything to do with them. Don't take it personally: let it repel off you. Don't give them your precious time or energy.

Instead, continue to do what is true for you and just be your beautiful, authentic self.

Remove yourself from that which is no longer serving you, with understanding in your heart.

I think it's also very important that women, particularly, set ourselves some healthy boundaries. Our conditioning means we are givers and nurturers. Men are just as naturally giving; however, we ladies are carefully taught to boost that tendency, while little boys are rewarded for being tough and ambitious. This is why women tend to overdeliver, so setting some healthy boundaries is necessary in order to master your Mean Girl and become wildly wealthy, fabulously healthy, and bursting with love. Remember, saying yes to others can mean saying no to yourself, and you must always put yourself first. If you aren't overflowing within yourself you are no good to your children, friends, boss, partner, family . . . or anyone, for that matter.

It's time to set some healthy boundaries; here's how:

1. *Get honest with yourself.*

    What are you doing that isn't really your truth but you're doing it because you think you "should"? Maybe it's looking over your colleague's report when he or she asks even though you're snowed under. Or babysitting your sister's kids even though you're up to your eyeballs in housework and deadlines. Or agreeing to a dinner date with your girlfriend when you know you really just need a quiet night at home. Doing things for others is nice, and sometimes saying yes to something can bring unexpected joy, but only if it's coming from love and doesn't sacrifice your health and happiness. By all means be helpful, but do it because you want to, not because you think you *"should."*

2. *Lovingly communicate from your heart.*

Before I got really serious in my business (and life, for that matter) it was acceptable for my girlfriends to call me during the day for hour-long chats. Now, on the other hand, this is an absolute no-go. One girlfriend in particular really struggled to get her head around this until I lovingly communicated from my heart why I could no longer chat for an hour in the middle of the day. Instead of getting frustrated with others, practice clear communication from your heart. It always works!

3. *Set boundaries for yourself too.*

It's all well and good to set boundaries with your friends, family members, and team, but what about setting some healthy boundaries for yourself? For me when I walk in the door after work at night, it's family time. I take off my boss-lady hat and slip into my wife and stepmama roles (roles I love so much). No jumping back on my laptop (unless it's an emergency), no work talk (this is a hard one), and no TV. Being an entrepreneur and a business owner calls for me to step into my ambitious, stronger energy a little more during the day—big decisions have to be made and this requires me to step up. Sometimes I struggle to shake off that business feel when I walk in the door, so I go and take a bath with Epsom salts and coconut oil and slip into more comfortable clothing. This helps me drop back into my softer side.

Another great boundary you can set for yourself and your family is no screens in the bedroom. The bedroom is reserved for sleeping and lovemaking only. No eating in bed, no watching TV, and definitely no laptops. If you use your phone as your alarm, get a sun lamp. Your bedroom is your sacred space and needs to be treated that way.

On that note, if you're serious about becoming wildly wealthy, fabulously healthy, and bursting with love I invite you to stop watching reality TV, reading trashy mags, and listening to talkback radio. They are not serving your higher good. Instead of watching TV, watch inspiring TED talks online. Instead of reading trashy mags, read soulful books that inspire you. And instead of listening to talkback radio, try some empowering podcasts. Break the habit and your soul will thank you.

Inspo-action

What are some healthy boundaries you need to set with others? Write down three.

_____

_____

_____

Now think about some healthy boundaries you can set with yourself. Maybe it's no screens after eight p.m., no TV in the mornings, or no more scrolling Instagram or checking e-mails as soon as you wake up. Write down three.

_____

_____

_____

Now remember, *insight without action is pointless*, so make sure you do whatever you need to do to help cement these new boundaries, both with others and yourself.

Closing the Door on Fear

Don't let the fear of what other people think of you stop you from following your heart.

A few years ago, one of my clients, Chloe, really wanted to start an online fashion store. She was so passionate about it, you could see the sparkle in her eyes every time she spoke about it. One day, she ran into an old friend at the post office and they started chatting about what they were each up to. Chloe mentioned her exciting new business idea and how she couldn't wait to get the ball rolling. Her "friend" almost spat out her coffee and told her that opening an on-line fashion store in the middle of a recession was ludicrous, and that no one likes to shop online because they like to be able to try things on. Immediately Chloe's heart sank. She cried the whole way home. I got an e-mail from her a few days later saying she had de-cided to dump the whole idea. She canceled the meeting with her Web designer and didn't think there was any point working with me anymore. I called her up, and she answered the phone sounding defeated. She began to give me a list of reasons why the online fashion store was no longer a great idea, repeating her friend's negative opinions and then some.

Sensing that something was amiss, I told her to close her eyes and take a few deep breaths. I then asked her to connect with how she was feeling right then. She said she felt tight, rigid, heavy, defeated, and angry. I invited her to envision her online store and how it would feel to have that as her business, how she would feel if that was what she put all her creative energy into each day. She said she felt excited, bursting with energy, with tingling goose bumps all over her body. I reminded her that *that was her truth*. Her fears were simply getting in the way of her seeing it. She was so excited to be back in touch with her truth that after we got off the phone, she called back her Web designer to reschedule their meeting. She later e-mailed me sharing that all the doubt and fear had come to her when she ran into her old "friend" at the post office and that she had soaked up all her friend's negativity.

As social creatures, we humans *love* to be heard. We love to give our opinion about *everything*, from what toothpaste to buy and which university to attend through to what diet is best for you and what we think the weather will be like on Saturday. But we need to learn to let go of others' opinions. Don't let *their* stuff get you down, and especially don't let it affect your life or business decisions.

Our Mean Girl is constantly looking for recognition, a pat on the back, and a big gold star of approval. I teach my team to stand strong in their decisions and not to look to me for a high five and a "well done" every time they've finished a task. I want to train them to feel fearless in their choices. This is how you create an amazing work culture.

Men are not taught to have this issue as much: many of them are therefore better able to make a decision and go for it one hundred percent—a trait I am trying to embody more.

I see this a lot with the mamas I have worked with in the past. Motherhood is a whole new world and a great opportunity for your Mean Girl to put you through the wringer and do some serious damage. It all starts with the well-intentioned advice about what you "should" and "shouldn't" do during pregnancy, then goes into childbirth, then mothers' group, and so on. Everyone wants to add their two cents and all you're trying to do is trust your intuition. Stay firmly rooted in *your* beliefs and do what feels right for *you. Remember, as a mama, what is truly right for you is what's right for your bubba too.* Stand confident in your choices.

Inspo-action

Are there areas in your life where you are looking for a pat on the back and a "well done"? Write them down.

_____

_____

_____

Remember, this is just your Mean Girl playing her sneaky little games. Stay grounded in *your* truth and you will never go wrong.

Being Resilient

*The strongest oak tree of the forest is not the one that is
protected from the storm and hidden from the sun, but it is the
one that stands in the open, where it is compelled to struggle for
its existence against the winds and rains and the scorching sun.*

ॐ NAPOLEON HILL

Resilience is the ability to go through adversity in such a way that
you come out the other side strengthened and better off for the experience. Being resilient means facing life's difficulties (and there
will be some) head-on with courage and patience, refusing to back
down and play the victim. *Resilience is staring your Mean Girl in
the eyes and saying: I see you, but I am not willing to let you win.* It's
scary—it takes serious courage—but it's this exact quality that allows
someone to rebound quickly from hardship, misfortune, or trauma
with insight and growth.

Being resilient takes practice and courage.

Resilience is not something we are born with; it is something
that is developed and strengthened as we grow and experience life.
To build your resilience muscle you must regularly put yourself in
the arena to battle it out. Playing it safe by getting cozy with your
Mean Girl and sticking to your comfort zone won't cut it.

The opposite of being resilient is feeling powerless and
victimized—which I felt for many years. When you're in that space,
it's easy to lean toward unhealthy coping mechanisms like drugs,
alcohol, excessive exercising habits, harmful relationships, or un-

healthy eating behaviors. On top of all that, when we feel like help-less victims, we allow our Mean Girls to take over and totally run the show.

I've certainly become more resilient over the years, but I've had to work at it. It's an ongoing process, and can take a lot of ballsiness, but it has made a massive difference in my life.

Here are some great ways to build your resilience muscle:

- **Flex your self-love muscle daily.** By doing this, you are enhancing your ability to bounce back.
- **Do something each day from your self-love menu.** By doing this, you're less likely to fall victim to your circumstances.
- **Take time for stillness.** Meditation twice a day helps you cultivate an inner groundedness, perfect for times when life throws you a curveball. I honestly don't think I would have been able to cope with my best friend passing away without meditation.
- **Get connected and ask for support.** Having a solid support network around you is imperative to help you bounce back from life's curveballs. You could even start seeing an energetic healer or kinesiologist or hire a spiritual coach to support you in moving through the adversity. Or try telling three of your closest friends or family members that you need a little extra support and love. Remember, asking for help is not a sign of weakness. Suffering alone in silence is.
- **Get crystal clear on your mission.** Knowing your

purpose and mission in life allows you to keep everything in perspective during times of adversity.

ₑ **Accept what is.** You cannot change what has happened in the past, but you can choose not to let it affect you anymore. By consciously accepting and letting go, you automatically free yourself from carrying this baggage with you into the future. Yes, some things will be easier to let go of than others, and you may need differing amounts of support and guidance for the harder times, but start to make the conscious effort within yourself to let go and go from there.

ₑ **Look for the deeper lesson.** There is a hidden message in every circumstance. Our job is to find it. Allow yourself to feel the heartache (or whatever feelings arise), but also ask yourself: "What did I learn throughout this experience?" Use the past as a tool of creation and not a weapon of mass destruction.

ₑ **Get deep sleep.** When you're tired, you're an easy target for your Mean Girl. Allow yourself more sleep than usual to help with the healing process.

ₑ **Move your body.** Doing yoga or Pilates or walking in nature has incredible physical and emotional benefits. It releases endorphins (feel-good hormones) in the body, which diminish the perception of pain.

ₑ **Nourish your temple.** In times of adversity, you must up the ante with your nutrition. Nourish yourself with fresh whole foods and filtered water to help support your body and nervous system.

Remember, resilience is a muscle that needs to be worked. It's all about stepping up and standing strong instead of falling victim to your Mean Girl.

Inspo-action

When in your life have you faced adversity and pushed through? Was it, for example, during a breakup, the loss of a job, or when you had a fight with a friend?

_____

_____

_____

_____

Now think of a time when you faced adversity and you didn't step up, playing the victim and choosing to suffer instead?

_____

_____

_____

_____

Reflect how these made you feel in your body. Which made you expand and which made you contract? It's super important to notice and feel the difference so that you can become even more aware of yourself and your body.

You have the power to choose how you respond to all situations in your life—not your mum, your partner, or your Mean Girl, _you_! So next time life throws you a curveball, put on your resilience raincoat and know that on the other side of the discomfort is always growth.

The Pity Party Dance-off

I used to play the victim role very well (like, on an Oscar-worthy level!) because I struggled with how to deal with my feelings. Whenever sadness, anger, or frustration arose within me, I didn't really know how to deal with it. So I simply suppressed it—as you now know, this is not the best idea!

I was always searching for the tools to deal with my feelings, but I'd never found anything that clicked. Until one day, I came up with the "pity party dance-off."

Having a pity party dance-off allows you to experience feelings fully and then let them go.

Here's how it works:

STEP 1: Whenever any unsettling feeling or emotion arises, immediately allow yourself to feel it. Go into a private room: the bathroom, the stockroom at your work, a broom closet, or your kitchen pantry. Any private spot where you can be alone and fully express yourself will work fine.

STEP 2: Once you enter the room, set the timer on your phone for approximately ten to fifteen minutes (depending on the severity of your feelings).

STEP 3: Once the timer starts, allow yourself to fully express *exactly* how you are feeling in the moment. Maybe you need to cry, scream into a pillow, punch the air vigorously, jump up and down, shake out your entire body, or simply sit in complete stillness and just breathe deeply.

Please note: you will intuitively know exactly what to do in that moment. Tune in and listen to your heart and body.

STEP 4: Fully feel and express yourself until the timer goes off.

STEP 5: Once the timer goes off and you have fully allowed yourself to feel and express everything inside you, place your hands over your heart and repeat this to yourself a few times:

"[Insert your name], I love you and you are safe. You can now let this go and move on."

STEP 6: Then, blast out your favorite upbeat track on your phone. I love Rihanna's "Diamonds" (it always makes me feel like a superstar!), Katy Perry's "Roar," or anything by Beyoncé. Proceed to dance your heart out. Bonus points if you sing along as loudly as you possibly can (caution: probably not the best idea if you're in the stockroom at your work!). But nevertheless, this will instantly snap you out of your funk.

I personally have found this to be the absolute *best* technique for allowing myself to quickly move through feelings and not waste a whole day (or week . . . or month) having a pity party for myself like I used to. Because let's face it: stuff is *always* going to come up in our lives. But this technique allows you to fully feel it, then let it go and move on.

When Jess passed on, I allowed myself the space of two weeks to fully and completely grieve. Of course I allowed myself to cry after that (and still do), but I really needed that space to just be. I didn't work for that period; all I did was sit with my emotions. I journaled, spoke to her, wrote her letters, sat in nature, and sobbed like a baby in my husband's arms. I was totally raw and vulnerable and allowed whatever needed to come out to flow. I welcomed all the pain with wide-open arms—I invited the frustration, anger, denial, sadness, isolation, depression, and heartache because I knew deep down it was all part of the process. And although the pain was immense, I didn't resist; I let it flow through me without judgment.

This was the first time in my life I had experienced a death of someone so close and, looking back, I am so grateful I had the tools to move through it with grace. This doesn't mean I still don't feel sadness, anger, or frustration—I absolutely do. As I sit here and write this my heart hurts, it feels heavy, and tears are welling in my eyes. I miss my best friend so much and still can't believe I won't get to hear her laugh again. It truly sucks! But the truth is, there is nothing I can do about it. All I can do is take the beautiful lessons she championed and continue to be inspired by her bravery, greatness, and ability to live life to its fullest.

And let it be said, yes—my Mean Girl *did* rear her head during this time, planting doubt and regret. She told me I should have called more, I should have made more time to see Jess, I should have given her that jumper of mine that she loved so much (!), but then I stopped and reminded myself that everything is perfect. Our friendship was like no other—it was beautiful, special, unique, and something I am so deeply grateful I got to experience. So I didn't need to let my Mean Girl take over. I gently closed the door on her and returned to my heart.

I don't think we ever get used to the fact that someone has passed on; we just get better at coping day to day with them no longer being here in the physical form. And eventually, instead of wishing it was another way, you feel grateful for the precious moments you did get to share.

So even if you are struck down by an intensely strong emotion like grief, don't run off with your Mean Girl. Sit with it, have a pity party dance-off if you wish, and know that this too shall pass. Whatever you are feeling is temporary and all part of the healing process.

Your Gift to the World Recap

- Never underestimate the potency and power of simply being you.
- Remember, everyone has an opinion and that's okay.
- What other people think of you is none of your business.
- Don't let the fear of what other people think of you stop you from following your heart.
- Resilience means staring your Mean Girl in the eyes and saying, *I see you, but I am not willing to let you win.*
- Being resilient takes practice and courage.
- Asking for help is not a sign of weakness. Suffering alone in silence is.

the art of letting go

Resentment is like drinking poison and then
hoping it will kill your enemies.

ANONYMOUS

Some people squeeze toothpaste from the bottom of the tube, whereas others squeeze it from the top.

Some people like the toilet roll to go on the holder with the paper hanging down from the front, whereas others like it to hang from the back.

Some people like to eat their Oreo cookies by taking a big bite, whereas others like to pry the bikkies apart and scoop out the goop within.

And you know what? In each of these situations, whatever our own beliefs are, we all like to think that the people who do it differently from us are wrong. W-r-o-n-g. In fact, I'm sure that there have literally been hundreds of thousands of fights—even marriages that have broken down—due to niggling resentment over "She squeezed the toothpaste wrong" and "He never hung the toilet roll right."

So who is right and who is wrong? Who needs to forgive who here, and who needs to "learn their lesson"?

The answer is, neither is right or wrong and no one needs to forgive anyone.

I am about to drop a massive truth-bomb on you, and I am well aware that you may judge me for what I am about to say, I may lose you, and it goes against what most personal development/self-help authors say, but, hold tight, tiger . . .

There is no such thing as forgiveness.

Bear with me.

My aim in life is to live judgment free, and saying someone else is wrong and I am right, or vice versa, is a big fat judgment and only creates obstacles for my growth. Nothing is right nor wrong, it just *is*! Until I label it as right or wrong.

Instead I prefer to use the words "letting go" and choose to remind myself that everyone is on different operating systems. The examples I just gave might seem a little silly—surely no one gets that worked up over toothpaste, right?—but their almost-trivial nature helps us to really see the truth of the situation: truly, no one is right; truly, we each are just operating with different belief systems. And if we can all have such staunch (and opposing) convictions over something as simple as dental hygiene, imagine how stubborn we can get over something we *actually* think is important, or when we think someone has "wronged" us.

Letting go and understanding we are all on different operating systems are the key to your freedom. This is an area that many people struggle with, usually because they have been holding on to pain, anger, and resentment for many years—sometimes their whole lives. But even though the practice can be confronting, letting go and understanding are two of the most powerful tools for your personal growth and essential if you truly want to live a life that's bursting with love.

> ## Soul Share
>
> Letting go and understanding are an act of
> self-love and the key to your freedom.

Ultimately, letting go is a choice between remaining stuck in the past and moving forward toward your dream life. When you let go, you are freeing yourself from the negative energy that's been holding you back. But when you refuse to let go and you fail to understand that others are programmed differently (no one better than any other), you're actually latching on to your hurt and weighing yourself down with suffering.

The reason many people struggle with letting go is because they think it means they are condoning the other person's behavior. That is absolutely not the case! Letting go does not mean condoning what happened. In fact, it has nothing to do with them and everything to do with you. The entire act of letting go takes place wholly within *you*—you're simply freeing yourself from the entrapment and accepting what is. This is why letting go and understanding are the keys to your freedom—they're the only way to keep your energy flowing freely and to move forward without baggage.

To get the full benefits of letting go, you need to practice it regularly. You have to let go of the judgment and feel understanding deep in your heart. Not just when it's easy or when it suits you either: always.

START WITH YOURSELF

You can practice letting go with yourself first: when you overeat, when you lose it at the person who cut you off in traffic, when you sleep in and miss yoga, when you don't finish everything on your to-do list, when you yell at your kids, when you get angry because your partner didn't take out the rubbish, and when someone doesn't meet your expectations. Seriously, practice it everywhere.

BUT WHAT ABOUT WHEN YOU'VE BEEN *REALLY* HURT?

I can hear you saying, "But, Melissa, how can you say that I should let go and have understanding for the person who abused me or cheated on me or broke my heart? That person doesn't *deserve* it!"

That's a perfectly normal reaction, but remember it's still a judgment and we've all felt that way at some point or another, but there's something you need to know: if you hold on to being "wronged," the resentment, sadness, and anger—whatever it is—will fester inside you and eat away at your soul.

The important thing to remember here is that we must take responsibility for ourselves. When we blame others for our misery, we are giving away our power and allowing the suffering to continue. Letting go and understanding are an incredibly potent way of taking that power back and moving forward with your life.

How to Let Go

STEP 1

If you have had a fight with a friend, got angry with your child, or given the finger to someone who cut you off at a traffic light, to start the process, remind yourself you are making a judgment by saying someone else is wrong and you are right. Then ask yourself, "How did I contribute to this situation? What role did I play?" Remember, it takes two to tango—you now know the importance of taking responsibility if you want to have divine relationships, and here is a perfect place to put that into practice. Also take a moment to consider the lesson that might underlie the situation at hand. Once you have found a deeper meaning behind what's happened, it's easier to let go and move on.

Looking back, when my ex-boyfriend cheated on me and I felt like my heart had been ripped out of my chest, there was a big lesson I needed to learn: I hadn't been owning my worth or standing in my power. At that time in my life, my worthy-o-meter was at zero, which was reflected in all areas of my life, especially my relationship. No wonder it played out the way it did.

Same goes for when I hit rock bottom. I had to do a lot of healing work around that time in my life, mainly on myself. Even though that was one of the toughest periods I have ever been through, I don't regret it at all. I am very grateful for that experience because it taught me so many valuable lessons and has led me to where I am today.

Regret is another form of fear. Your Mean Girl will use it to keep you locked in the past.

STEP 2

The next step is to send that person love. I know what you're thinking: "How on earth can I send the person who hurt me *love*? That person certainly doesn't deserve my *love*!" But one of the biggest spiritual lessons I have ever learned is that *everyone is always doing the very best they can with their knowledge and understanding at any given time*. Invariably, someone who has mistreated you was mistreated at some point in their own life—most likely as a child—and the greater the violence, the greater their own inner pain. *Meet them with understanding in your heart.* And remember, everyone is on different operating systems. No one is better than anyone else: they're just different. Having awareness that they too have suffered and felt pain helps contextualize their journey and is essential for our own growth.

HOW TO SEND SOMEONE LOVE

Simply close your eyes and envision that person standing in front of you. Look them in the eyes. Now imagine white light pouring out of your heart and into theirs. This white light is pure love, and it is incredibly healing and powerful. If emotions come up, just allow them to flow, and keep pouring love until you feel neutral. This may take some time, so be patient.

"But what if I can't do it? What if the pain is too unbearable?" I hear you, sister! I really struggled with this at first, but do not underestimate the potency of this exercise. This one action will transform your internal GPS and allow you to truly become bursting with love. If you're skeptical, at least give it a go and see how you feel. Be aware that your Mean Girl will want immediate proof, but this is one of those many examples in life where it's the little things you do each day that add up to big results.

STEP 3

Once we've figured out our lesson and have sent the other person love, it's time to let go.

The ancient Egyptians believed that after a person died, his or her soul was measured on a sacred scale. It was weighed against the "feather of truth"—if the soul was lighter than the feather, the deceased could freely journey onward into the blissful afterlife. But if the soul was heavier than the feather—weighed down by anger, regrets, resentment, and bitterness—then the soul would return to earth and live another lifetime. The cycle would keep repeating until the soul could finally learn to let go of those heavy, negative emotions and be free.

This ancient myth is a powerful reminder to let go of all the emotional burdens we carry around with us—the pain, anger, sadness, resentment—anything that is no longer serving us and that's stopping us from being fully present. And the best way to make sure we have a feather-light soul? Yep, you know it: letting go.

I know it can seem like getting to that place of release within yourself might be miles away, but all you have to do is begin where you are. Just start with one little baby step toward letting go of anger, sadness, judgment, pain, or resentment. You will be amazed at how a couple of tiny, bite-size steps can snowball into a giant internal shift.

You might also encounter a situation where you *think* you have fully let go of a situation, but then something happens that triggers your hurt and pain all over again. If this happens, don't despair; don't feel like you've undone all your hard work. It's just another spiritual assignment for you to master and another layer of heaviness for you to shed. You simply need to keep letting go, releasing the pain, and see where it takes you. This process of becoming "lighter" is "en-*light*-enment."

Practicing letting go and understanding results in radical shifts.

When you embark on a journey of nonjudgment and letting go within yourself, other people can feel it. They can intuitively sense a shift within you, even if they can't articulate it. This is because you are now vibrating at a higher level and your whole energy field has lifted: a surefire sign of personal growth.

Sometimes, at this stage, people choose to tell the person—either verbally or through a letter—that they've let go and found understanding in their heart. This might be supportive for you, but it's by no means essential. In fact, sometimes it's better for the entire process to be conducted on the inside. Regardless of what feels right to you, your energy field will change because of your letting-go work—you'll feel lighter, space will open up inside you, and you'll be open to receiving wonderful things from the Universe.

To be honest, it took me many years to let go and find understanding in my heart for my ex, but when I finally realized I was judging him and he was doing the very best he could at that point in his life, it was like a massive weight had been lifted off my shoulders. I felt like I could finally *breathe* again—it was incredibly liberating. I told no one but was privately blown away by how good it felt. Then something quite phenomenal happened: a few months later, out of the blue, I received an e-mail from him profusely apologizing for his behavior. He explained how he had been hurt in the past and how he had taken it out on me. He also mentioned how grateful he was for our time together and that he was sending me love. I felt totally neutral reading his e-mail, then a wave of love washed over me. I wrote back thanking him for his e-mail, and I told him that I too was grateful for our time together. We were both able to close that chapter of our lives for good—we haven't spoken since—and move forward with nothing but wholehearted love in our hearts for each other. It really is a beautiful thing.

Letting Go and Accepting Thyself

The most important person you need to stop judging and to let off the hook is yourself. When I was lying in the hospital I was so *angry*—angry with the world, angry with the people around me, but most of all, angry with myself. Even though I felt enormous resistance, I started doing some acceptance work on myself. Every day in the hospital I would place my hands over my heart and repeat,

"I love you and I accept exactly what is," over and over. Heck, I had nothing else to do, so I thought I may as well give it a shot!

And it worked! Those simple words triggered an enormous shift inside me. Of course, I had to be persistent and really keep at it. In fact, I still do this exercise whenever I feel I need it, usually when I am driving. Driving is a great place to repeat affirmations—turn off the trashy radio and start repeating your affirmations.

I have also found affirmations and mirror work together very transformational. Even if you don't believe the affirmation right away, keep at it. We have to reprogram the negative thought patterns and create new ones and this process takes time.

Here are some of my favorite self-love affirmations:

- I love you and I accept exactly what is.
- I give myself permission to let go of the pain from the past. I no longer need to hold on.
- You are safe; I can now let go.
- I release the past so I can step into the future with intention and purpose.
- I am worthy of all the love life has to offer.
- I gently release all anger and resentment and return to my heart.
- The past is no longer relevant; I choose to be in the present moment.
- Each moment in every breath is a fresh start, a clean slate, a new beginning.
- I am free to be me and share my gifts with the world.

↩ I release my need to be "perfect."

↩ I no longer need to hold on to the past.

Doing these affirmations while staring in the mirror is seriously powerful, but you can also say them while you're driving, doing the dishes, in the shower, or getting dressed in the morning. Pick one and start repeating it over and over. Remember, even if you don't one hundred percent believe it at the beginning, please keep at it. Try to connect with the words and really *feel* them vibrate through your entire body. This work does get easier, but only if you commit to doing it daily.

The most important thing with letting go is to make sure it's not too serious. Make it as light as you can. When you stuff up and fall down, giggle at yourself, say, "Oopsy daisy," and pick yourself back up again. You wouldn't scream at a two-year-old if she fell over: you would encourage her to pick herself back up and try again. Try not to dwell and make things more dramatic than they need to be. We humans have a tendency to catastrophize things, especially in our minds. Let it go and move on as quickly as you can while recognizing whatever needs to be acknowledged within you.

And the final word on letting go: keep on going, no matter what. Even when it's tough, even when you don't think you can, and even when you feel shattered on the inside. I promise you, if you stop judging, let go, and find understanding and acceptance deep in your heart, you'll be blown away by the internal shifts it creates in your life.

Inspo-action

What are you currently holding on to that you need to let go of?

_____

_____

_____

_____

_____

In your daily meditation practice, choose someone or a situation you want to let go of. Go through the three steps for letting go, and focus on pouring love from your heart to theirs. Stick with that one person until you feel you have released the pain—you might have to stay with them for a week, a month, or even longer. Just keep at it until you have completely let go and freed yourself.

Remember, _insight without inspired action is pointless_, so take action now! Commit to letting these things go so that you can master your Mean Girl and live your best life.

The Art of Letting Go Recap

- Forgiveness is a judgment.
- Letting go and understanding are the keys to your freedom.
- Letting go and understanding are an act of self-love.

- When you practice nonjudgment, letting go and understanding—whether it's for someone else or yourself—you are freeing yourself from pain and releasing the energy that you have been holding on to.
- Everyone is on different operating systems and is always doing the very best they can with their knowledge and understanding at any given time.
- Meet others with understanding in your heart.

TEN

be a trailblazer.
live your legacy.

We're here for a reason. I believe a bit of the
reason is to throw little torches out to
lead people through the dark.

WHOOPI GOLDBERG

All my life I have felt different. In primary school, I so desperately
wanted to fit in, but all the girls liked sports and I liked dancing. In
high school, I tried to fit in by getting good grades, but all I wanted
was to be on stage. In my early twenties, I tried to fit in and be cool
by drinking and partying, even though I didn't really enjoy it. All of
it was exhausting and *not* my truth. I can't help but look back and
feel a twinge in my heart for that little girl, so desperately wanting to
fit in and feel accepted. If I could go back in time, I would tell her
that she is perfect exactly the way she is.

From a young age, we are taught to conform and fit in. Our culture likes to slot us into tidy boxes with convenient labels. If some-

one stands out, they are pushed straight back down; their gifts and uniqueness are not nurtured and they're definitely not celebrated.

But this is not the way I want and choose to live. It keeps our truth trapped inside of us and stops us shining our true light. *If we really want to start living to our full potential and sharing all our incredible gifts with the world, we must start celebrating our uniqueness, not suppressing it.*

I see this a lot with Leo's school, which is why we make sure to celebrate his uniqueness a lot at home. We let him express himself any way he likes. Sometimes that's through dancing, singing, sports, playing the piano or violin, painting, creating a masterpiece with Lego, or solving a Rubik's Cube in less than ten seconds (true story . . . the kid is a genius!). We have always encouraged Leo to do what's true for him and to follow his feelings. He goes to a very sporty all-boys' school and although he chooses to participate in sports, he also loves to express himself creatively through dance, singing, art, and music. Once he came home with a letter to say that he was performing in the school choir the following Sunday—we didn't even know he had joined the choir! We asked if any of his friends were doing it and he said no, he "just felt like doing it." We've always encouraged him to do what's true for him, so he naturally just tuned in to his truth, followed his feelings, and didn't care what anyone else thought.

That sort of commitment to your truth is what we are all aiming for. And if Leo can do it, so can we fully fledged adults!

Being a trailblazer comes down to not caring what other people think. We spoke about it before, but it really is the bedrock to living your wildest dreams. I know it's not easy, I know it takes courage, but it's oh so rewarding when you do.

Stepping Outside Your Comfort Zone

Hanging out in your comfort zone is cozy. I get it—I hung out in mine for years! It's warm in there. It feels safe and secure and you feel in control. But if you always hang out with your Mean Girl in your comfort zone, you can never upgrade your internal operating system and evolve. And deep down you know there's no real comfort in this zone at all.

In the past, I used to be petrified of exiting my comfort zone, to the point where I didn't even like leaving the house. I hated the thought of not being in control and I especially didn't like the fact that I couldn't control what I was going to eat when I was out (yep, recovering control freak, right here!). I would go to great lengths not to put myself in any situations I couldn't control. I built up a sturdy perimeter around me and just hung out in there where it felt safe.

These days, I love getting out of my comfort zone. Don't get me wrong, I still feel scared and my Mean Girl rears her head from time to time, but it's that exact feeling that makes me feel alive. Seriously, if your current goals or projects at work don't scare the bejesus out of you just a little bit, then you're not dreaming big enough.

I get that rush of fear every time I'm about to step out on stage to speak. My body heats up, my palms become sweaty, and my heart begins to race. This is how I know something is important to me—if it wasn't it wouldn't affect me. Fear is a good indicator you're on the right track.

Relinquishing that sense of control is a tricky thing to do at first. After all, controlling is one of your Mean Girl's default settings. It keeps you trapped in fear, makes you paralyzed with uncertainty, and lets her run the show. Know that if you want to master your Mean Girl, you must be aware of the areas in your life where you are trying to force things, and you must actively decide to lay down the reins and let go.

Why do we try to control things?

Here are three reasons we get our control freak on:

1. **We try to control things because of what we *think* will happen.** We fear the unknown and tend to imagine the worst. Rationally, we know that what we think *might* happen will probably never happen. But despite this deep-down knowingness (which is our truth), we choose to ignore it and try to control the outcome anyway.

2. **We are attached to the outcome, so we try to control the here and now.** I used to try to control everything in my life—from what I put in my mouth to how others perceived me—because I was so hell-bent on a specific outcome (like being thin or "well liked"). But it's not until you let go of the outcome that things actually start to fall into place. For example, as soon as I let go of my "lose weight or else" agenda and started nourishing my body, the excess weight slowly started falling off naturally, and it has stayed off without me going on crazy yo-yo lemon detox diets and taking fat-loss pills.

3. **We think surrendering to change leads to a scary unknown.** This sees us holding on with a white-knuckle grip to everything that's familiar and safe, in order to preserve the status quo. But the thing is, when we let go and surrender, we actually open ourselves up to possibilities that might not have shown up were we still busy trying to control the future.

When we have our control-freak hat on and things don't pan out the way we want, we start to lose it. Basically, shit hits the fan and our whole life stinks. But if you weren't being a control freak in the first place, you could have opened yourself up to life unfolding whichever way it was meant to unfurl. And you'd end up feeling a whole lot calmer, saner, and more loving in the process.

A case in point for me was two weeks before my wedding, when the catering company we'd booked pulled out. We made one phone call and *boom*: it was all sorted. The old me would have handled that situation very differently—after I freaked out, had a panic attack, and wiped the anxiety sweat from my brow, I likely would have cursed down the phone at the caterers, told them they were wrong for doing this to me two weeks before my wedding, and then hung up in a rage. But seriously, what good is that going to do for anyone? Instead, I put my big-girl pants on and told myself that **everything happens for a reason**. After I made one phone call, we ended up hiring the people who we originally wanted to use but who weren't available at the time, but now magically were. You see, everything always works out exactly the way it's supposed to, and the sooner you realize that, the sooner you'll master your Mean Girl.

Living Your Truth

As soon as you feel yourself conforming, step out of that box. Connect with your truth and do what feels right for *you*.

When you deny your truth there is always a consequence.

Standing out and being different isn't easy. It forces you to be your authentic self, it leaves you vulnerable, and it can make you feel like you're naked on a stage in front of a packed audience. But having to deal with the discomfort far outweighs the alternative. Like I mentioned before, when you suppress your truth, it festers inside you and manifests negativity in your life and body. Which can show up as a disease, illness, addiction, or general unhappiness. And although it may not manifest immediately, eventually it will come up in some way, shape, or form. There's simply no escaping your truth.

Soul Share

The truth is relentless.

It's also important to share your truth with the loved ones around you, even if this leaves you feeling vulnerable. When I ask my friends how they are and they reply, "Yeah, good," in a total "I am really struggling right now" tone, I call them on it. I ask them to tell me how they *really* are. I am not here to have fake conversations or inauthentic relationships. I want the real deal, baby—not the fake version, where your Mean Girl runs the show.

Sharing your truth with people is beautiful, but also be mindful of *who* you share your story with. Remember, everyone is on different operating systems and not everyone is going to agree with you and your beliefs, and that's okay. Let your intuition guide you here. Feel if the other person is open and receptive to your truth; and, if not, don't waste your energy. For example, there are certain things I know my parents and I have different beliefs on and that's okay. I'm not going to force them to live my beliefs and I'm certainly not going to try to convince them every time I see them.

But is vulnerability and sharing your truth a sign of weakness? Absolutely not! It's a sign of strength, courage, and bravery. I bow down to you when you show up as the real you, as does everyone else.

Vulnerability makes people lean in.

Vulnerability is beautiful, raw, and truthful. And it's the secret to genuine connection and living your truth.

There is nothing more attractive and sexy than when someone is showing up as her true, authentic self.

Way too many women are terrified of showing their vulnerable sides. We're afraid of anyone thinking we're not "perfect." We think we have to do it all, we have to know all the answers, and we think that asking for help is a sign of weakness. Eventually, we start to develop a certain "toughness" around the edges in order to cope—we build up a thick skin, we harden our shell and lock off our hearts, and we become distanced from our true inner goddess.

This defensive mechanism we've built for ourselves is not serving us. It's just blocking us from our truth. We need to return home to our sacred feminine that oozes softness, tenderness, and openness—to the divine goddess who resides in us all. This doesn't mean you can't also be strong, dynamic, and compelling; it means your strength is grounded in owning your own power, not in acting and pretending like everything's okay.

"Being strong" or "holding it together" doesn't make you a better person. It only suppresses what's really going on. Being the true feminine goddess you are is your birthright. Let go of pretending and return to the truth of who you are.

Leaving a Legacy

If you would not be forgotten as soon as you are dead and rotten, either write things worth reading or do things worth the writing.

BENJAMIN FRANKLIN

We are here to give and be of service to the world. Ignoring your truth is a disservice to you and the planet. If today was your last day on earth, would you be happy with the imprint you left behind? Would you have left this place in better shape than you found it? What legacy are you leaving?

You don't have to be Mother Teresa to leave behind a legacy. You don't need to be a CEO or a famous scientist or a leader in your industry. By simply choosing love over fear and mastering your Mean

Girl, you are making an impact. Every single time you say yes to love, you are changing yourself, the people around you, and the planet as a whole. *You* are causing a ripple effect.

So let me ask you this ... How are you showing up? Right now, are you showing up as the fullest version of yourself? Or are you showing up as a cranky, half-full version? What you do in this moment matters and is shaping the story and message of your entire life.

Although I was brought to my knees (many times) by sadness, pain, and heartache when Jess passed on, I have also felt inspired—actually, blown away—by the beautiful legacy this woman has left behind. She has inspired millions of people all over the world simply by being her beautiful, unique, authentic self. She unapologetically lived her truth, and that is why I love her.

I knew Jess was an incredible influence on people's lives, but I guess when you are besties with someone, it's easy to become immune to just how huge their impact truly is. After I wrote an article on my website about her passing, I was filled with so much love and awe at how many souls she touched for the better. Through my tears, I read hundreds of comments, moved by the words that were pouring from people's hearts all over the world. I could feel their love through the computer screen and I felt an enormous sense of pride in calling her my soul sister.

This got me thinking about my own legacy: am I going to leave this earth in the best possible shape I can? Am I acting as my highest self in every moment? Am I showing up fully and completely in every moment? Am I being unapologetically me in each moment?

Or am I playing small? Limiting myself and letting my Mean Girl run the show?

Yet again, Jess is one of my biggest inspirations here and is constantly calling me to play higher every day. In moments of despair I can hear her voice saying, "Come on, Mel, you can do this, beautiful." I remember this one time we were standing in her kitchen drinking green juice (of course) and I had just found out that I'd landed my book deal with my dream publishers. I said to her, "My Mean Girl is telling me I can't do this. Did you ever have that?" And without a moment's hesitation she responded, "Nope! Why would you think that? We can do whatever we want!" That was typical Jess. She never doubted her ability, she never let her Mean Girl tell her she couldn't do anything, and she never played small. I love this about her.

The Collins Dictionary defines *legacy* as "something handed down or received from an ancestor or predecessor." However, I prefer this definition: legacy is about sharing what you have learned, not just what you have earned. Material wealth is only a small fraction of your true legacy—the rest of it lies in making genuine and lasting contributions to others and serving causes greater than yourself.

You don't just "create" a legacy and—*boom*—you're done with it. It's an ongoing activity that stretches on through all your days. And it's not something you create for profit or fame or recognition— although sometimes those things do come hand in hand with it. Your legacy actually stems out of a desire to contribute, to help, to create something greater than yourself and your life, something that will continue to serve the world . . . even after you've passed on.

So I pose this question to you on behalf of a planet that's hungry for the gifts that only you can share: what legacy are you creating right now?

When you ponder that question, maybe some things start to seem silly or insignificant. Like the fact that your kids point-blank refused to clean up their bedrooms before dinner or that your e-book design is taking a million years or that your partner left his wet towel on the floor *again*. In the big scheme of things, none of that really matters. It all comes back to being present and showing up fully in every moment as your best self. That's all we can ever do.

So what does your best self actually look like? It's helpful to consciously map it out. My best self is calm, grounded, present, patient, overflowing with love, honest, authentic, giving, loyal, and open, just for a start.

Inspo-action

What does your best self look like?

_____

_____

_____

_____

Head to my website and print out your Best Self Checklist and keep it somewhere you can see it, so you can constantly be reminded of your truth.

- Be brave, bold, and courageous, my sweet friend.
- Don't be afraid to think differently.
- Leap.
- Soar.

- Laugh hysterically.
- Love unconditionally.
- Play like a child.
- Give wholeheartedly.
- Be of service.
- Change the rules.
- Master your Mean Girl and blaze your own trail.
- The world is waiting for you to shine your light.

Inspo-action

Let's start "dreamlining." What do you want to leave behind in this world? What do you want your legacy to be? Picture your unique destiny, envision your end goal, and pour your heart onto the page. In the words of Zig Ziglar, "If you can dream it, you can achieve it."

_____

_____

_____

_____

_____

_____

_____

_____

_____

_____

Be a Trailblazer and Live Your Legacy Recap

- We must celebrate our uniqueness and not suppress it.
- Remember, everything happens for a reason.
- When you deny your truth there is always a consequence.
- Vulnerability makes people lean in. It's beautiful, raw, and truthful.
- There is nothing more attractive than when someone is unapologetically themselves.
- By simply choosing love over fear and mastering your Mean Girl, you are making an impact and leaving a legacy.

Bursting with Love Checklist

This final section of the book has helped you spread your wings and take flight on the journey toward creating a life bursting with white-hot love. The following affirmations will help you internalize what you've learned. As always, I encourage you to do whatever it takes to make sure you see them, remember them, and use them as much as possible—remember, it's in the *doing* that you'll experience the biggest shifts!

- ☐ The biggest gift I can give the world is to be my true, authentic self.
- ☐ I choose to let go of all past hurts.
- ☐ I choose to be a game changer and blaze my own trail.

a final note

The process of mastering your Mean Girl and creating the life of your dreams is not one that can merely be read about in a book. It must be lived. Experienced. Felt.

Now is the time for action, beautiful. Don't let this be just another book that you immerse yourself in, then cast aside so you can leap into the next one. If you are serious about change, you have to make it so; **if nothing changes, then nothing changes.**

Wherever you are on your journey, know that the Universe will support you in every step you take. Perhaps in ways you can't quite see yet, but trust that it's always on your side. You see, you are one of its divine children and it wants to see you shine.

So do the work, darling. Tune in to your truth, release your fears, and commit to tiny baby steps each and every day, and you will succeed in living a life beyond your wildest dreams.

And above all else, remember this:

Your true nature is love. Your potential is boundless. And your time is now.

You've got this, beautiful.

what's next?

Take the wisdom in these pages and let it percolate. Really sit with it, and remember, *insight without inspired action is useless*. It's now time to put everything you have read into some serious Mean Girl butt-kicking action. If you haven't downloaded all your free goodies from my website, head over and do that now: www.master ingyourmeangirl.com.

In order for a plant to grow you must water it, and I believe in order for our human consciousness to evolve we must water ourselves with knowledge. When you head to my website you will find out how you can continue to master your Mean Girl, how we can work together, and how you can stay on your path of evolution.

Want to join the tribe of epic trailblazing women? Come like my Facebook page (www.facebook.com/MelissaAmbrosiniTribe), follow me on Twitter (www.twitter.com/mel_ambrosini) and Instagram (www.instagram.com/melissaambrosini), and subscribe to my YouTube channel (www.youtube.com/MelissaAmbrosini)—and don't forget to leave me a comment and introduce yourself.

I can't wait to meet you.

bursting with gratitude . . .

There have been so many influential people in my life who have not only supported me on my journey but helped me birth *Mastering Your Mean Girl* into the world and for that I am eternally grateful. So, before the tears start to flow I want to first acknowledge *you*, my beautiful reader, for following your heart and picking up this book. Your spirit, your bravery, and your willingness to master your Mean Girl inspire me beyond measure. You are my biggest inspiration.

My divine husband. For constantly inspiring me to be the fullest version of myself. For holding me accountable and reminding me daily to master *my* Mean Girl. For encouraging me to be love in every moment. For being the most beautiful being (and business partner) to hold hands and walk this path with. For your unconditional love and support, and for being my biggest cheerleader. I love you endlessly.

To Leo, for gracing this planet with your presence. For showing me depths of love I didn't know existed. For teaching me about unconditional love. For reminding me to play and be present and for allowing my heart to burst with love every day.

To my parents, for always encouraging me to do what I love and follow my dreams. Thank you for your unconditional love and support: you guys are the *best*!

To my dreams in-laws, Ros and Grazie, not only for creating Nick but for being the unequivocal rock to us both. Thank you for expanding my heart and welcoming me into yours so openly.

To my soul sisters:

Jess Ainscough for inspiring me daily to be and give more. I miss you every single day and can't thank you enough for the imprint you have left deep in my heart.

Rachel MacDonald for your endless love, encouragement, and support. Our hour-long soul sessions fill my heart. Thank you for being such a beautiful example of pure love.

Cassie Waugh and Katie Ambrosini, my two "longest" friends, thank you for your friendship, unconditional love, and for always standing by my side.

To my dream sister-in-law, Emma: thank you for being you. You're perfect!

My epic team, especially Sam Shorter. Thank you times a billion for all your love and support and for sharing my mission with me.

Bayleigh Vedelago for your beautiful photography. Having you in my life and working with you is an absolute blessing.

Jess Larsen for your wicked word wizardry. Having you on the MA team is a gift.

My literary agent, Bill Gladstone, for believing in me.

Jake Ducey for your unconditional love and support and for inspiring me every single day.

Rachel MacDonald, Nina Karnikowski, Bhava Ram, Gemma

Davis, Graham Broadhurst, Dana Stephenson, Jess Ainscough, Carli Freiberg, Julie Parker, and Erika Lamour for being part of my epic reading council. Your feedback was invaluable.

To all my teachers and mentors, thank you for reminding me of the truth and guiding me back home to myself.

To my dream publishers, HarperCollins and Penguin Random House, and especially Catherine Milne and Andrew Yackira, you guys are heaven to work with. I am beyond grateful to create magic with you all.

And again to you, my darling reader, for having the courage to think a little differently. To step outside the box, to master your Mean Girl, and to live a life beyond your wildest dreams.

I bow to you!

Keep going, darling—you've got this!

You Only Live Once

You Only Live Once

Find Your Purpose. Reclaim Your Power.
Make Life Count.

NOOR HIBBERT

JOHN
MURRAY
LEARNING

First published in Great Britain by John Murray Learning in 2021
An imprint of John Murray Press
A division of Hodder & Stoughton Ltd,
An Hachette UK company

5

Copyright © Noor Hibbert 2021

A CIP catalogue record for this title is available from the British Library

Trade Paperback ISBN 978 1 529 37646 3
eBook ISBN 978 1 529 37647 0

Typeset by KnowledgeWorks Global Ltd.

Printed and bound in Great Britain by Clays Ltd, Elcograf S.p.A.

John Murray Press policy is to use papers that are natural, renewable and recyclable
products and made from wood grown in sustainable forests. The logging and manufacturing
processes are expected to conform to the environmental regulations of the country of
origin.

John Murray Press
Carmelite House
50 Victoria Embankment
London EC4Y 0DZ

www.johnmurraypress.co.uk

Dedication

This book is dedicated to my four children, Layla-Rose, Safia-Lily, Amira-Jasmine and my first son, who is growing in my belly as we speak.

Thank you for giving my life endless purpose and for teaching me to be a better person every day. Never ever ever settle for anything less than the dreams in your heart. Question everything and never accept anything less than what you desire. I love you with every cell in my body.

Acknowledgements

Thank you to my darling husband and love of my life Richard for allowing me to live my purpose and supporting me wholeheartedly. I'm so grateful we get to do this thing called life together.

Thank you to my agent Jessica, for continually believing in me and therefore allowing me to make the impact I desire.

Thank you to my editor Jonathan, for letting me be unapologetically me without judgement and for giving me the space to write this book how I wanted.

Thank you to my mother who reminds me every day how to love unconditionally and that anything is possible with the right mindset.

And to all my clients and followers that give me constant support and love – I wouldn't be here without you. I wrote this book for you.

Contents